SRA Art Connections

Level 3

Authors

Rosalind Ragans, Ph.D., Senior Author

Willis Bing Davis
Tina Farrell
Jane Rhoades Hudak, Ph.D.
Gloria McCoy
Bunyan Morris
Nan Yoshida

Contributing Writer

Marie Mennes

Music Center Education Division
The Music Center of Los Angeles County

SRA McGraw-Hill

Columbus, Ohio

A Division of The McGraw-Hill Companies

SRA/McGraw-Hill

A Division of The McGraw-Hill Companies

Copyright © 1998 by SRA/McGraw-Hill.

Send all inquiries to:
SRA/McGraw-Hill
8787 Orion Place
Columbus, OH 43240-4027

Printed in the United States of America.

ISBN 0-02-688317-1

6 7 8 9 VHP 04 03 02 01 00

Authors
Senior Author
Dr. Rosalind Ragans, Ph. D.
Associate Professor Emerita
Georgia Southern University

Willis Bing Davis
Art Department Chair
Central State University, Ohio

Tina Farrell
Director of Visual and Performing Arts,
Clear Creek, Independent School
District, Texas

Jane Rhoades Hudak, Ph.D.
Professor of Art
Georgia Southern University

Gloria McCoy
K–12 Art Supervisor, Spring Branch
Independent School District, Texas

Bunyan Morris
Demonstration Art Teacher
Marvin Pittman Laboratory School,
Georgia Southern University

Nan Yoshida
Former Art Supervisor,
Los Angeles Unified School
District, California

 **Contributors
ARTSOURCE Music,
Dance, Theater Lessons**
The Music Center of
Los Angeles County
Education Division,
Los Angeles, California
Executive Director, Music Center
Education Division–Joan Boyett
Concept Originator and
Project Director–Melinda Williams
Project Coordinator–
Susan Cambigue-Tracey
Arts Discipline Writers:
Dance–Susan Cambigue-Tracey
Music–Rosemarie Cook-Glover
Theater–Barbara Leonard
Staff Assistance–Victoria Bernal
Logo Design–Maureen Erbe

More About Aesthetics
Richard W. Burrows, Executive
Director, Institute for Arts Education,
San Diego, California

Safe Use of Art Materials
Mary Ann Boykin, Visiting Lecturer, Art
Education; Director, The Art School for
Children and Young Adults, University
of Houston-Clear Lake, Houston, Texas

Museum Education
Marilyn JS Goodman, Director of
Education, Solomon R. Guggenheim
Museum,
New York, New York

The National Museum of Women in the Arts Collection
National Museum of
Women in the Arts,
Washington, DC

Contributing Writer
Marie M. Mennes
Art Supervisor
Dade County Public Schools
Miami, FL

Reviewers
Mary Ann Boykin
Visiting Lecturer, Art Education;
Director, The Art School for Children
and Young Adults
University of Houston-Clear Lake
Houston, TX

Judy Gong
Multi-age Classroom Teacher
Pacific Elementary School
Lincoln Unified School District
Stockton, CA

Lori Groendyke Knutti
Art Educator
Harrison Street Elementary School
Big Walnut Elementary School
Sunbury, OH

Grace Baptiste-Hall
Elementary Teacher
42nd Street School
Los Angeles Unified School District
Los Angeles, CA

Nancy L. James
Third Grade Teacher
Dallas Public Schools
Dallas, TX

Steven R. Sinclair
Art Teacher
Big Country Elementary School
Southwest Independent School District
San Antonio, TX

Student Activity Testers
Molly McCloskey
Danielle Kintz
Kelley Krebs
Matthew Cohan
Kyle Harter

TABLE OF CONTENTS

Unit 1 — Line and Shape

Unit 2 — Color and Value

Table of Contents
(continued)

Unit 3 Space and Form

Unit 4 Balance and Emphasis

Table of Contents
(continued)

More About . . .

What Is Art?

Art is . . .

Painting

Painting is color applied to a flat surface.

Henri Matisse. (French). *Woman in Blue.* 1937. Oil on canvas. $36\frac{1}{2}$ x 29 inches. Philadelphia Museum of Art, Gift of Mrs. John Wintersteen/©1998 Succession H. Matisse. Paris/Artists Rights Society (ARS), New York.

Sculpture

Sculpture is art that fills up space.

Frederic Remington. (American). *Mountain Man.* 1903. Bronze. Carleton Private Collection.

Art is made by people

- to communicate ideas.
- to express feelings.
- to give us well-designed objects.

Drawing

Drawing is the process of making art with lines.

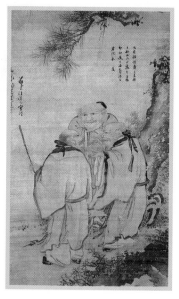

Wang Chao. (Chinese). *The Three Stars of Happiness, Wealth, and Longevity.* c. 1500. Hanging scroll. Ink and light colors on silk. $62\frac{1}{2}$ x $37\frac{1}{2}$ inches. Kimbell Art Museum, Fort Worth, Texas.

Architecture

Architecture is the art of designing and constructing buildings.

Artist unknown. (Greece). *Parthenon.* 447–438 B.C. Athens, Greece.

8

Printmaking

Printmaking is the process of transferring an original image from one prepared surface to another.

Thomas Hart Benton. (American). *I Got a Girl on Sourwood Mountain.* 1938. Lithograph. $12\frac{1}{2}$ x $9\frac{1}{4}$ inches. ©1988 T. H. Benton and R. P. Benton Testamentary Trusts/Licensed by VAGA, New York, NY. Courtesy of the Library of Congress, Washington, DC.

Photography

Photography is a technique of capturing an image of light on film.

Allen E. Cole. (American). *Silas Johnson.* 1920s. Hand-tinted photograph. Western Reserve Historical Society. The Allen E. Cole Collection. Cleveland, Ohio.

Pottery

Pottery is an object made from clay.

Artist unknown. (Chinese). *Covered Jar.* Ming Dynasty, Jiajing era. c. 1522-1566. Porcelain painted with underglaze cobalt blue and overglaze enamels. The Asia Society, New York, Mr. and Mrs. John D. Rockefeller 3rd Collection/Photo by Lynton Gardiner.

Mask

A mask is a covering for the face made by artists to be used in ceremonies, rituals, and other events.

Artist unknown. Abelam (Papua New Guinea). *Yam Mask.* Nineteenth century. Yam fibers. $18\frac{3}{4}$ x $13\frac{3}{8}$ inches. Nelson-Atkins Museum of Arts, Kansas City, Missouri.

. . . and much more.

Art is a language.

The words of the language are the elements of art.

Line

Line

Shape

ColoR

VALUE

SPACE

FORM

TEXTURE

Artists organize these words using the principles of art.

Rhythm

Balance

Emphasis

Variety

Harmony

Unity

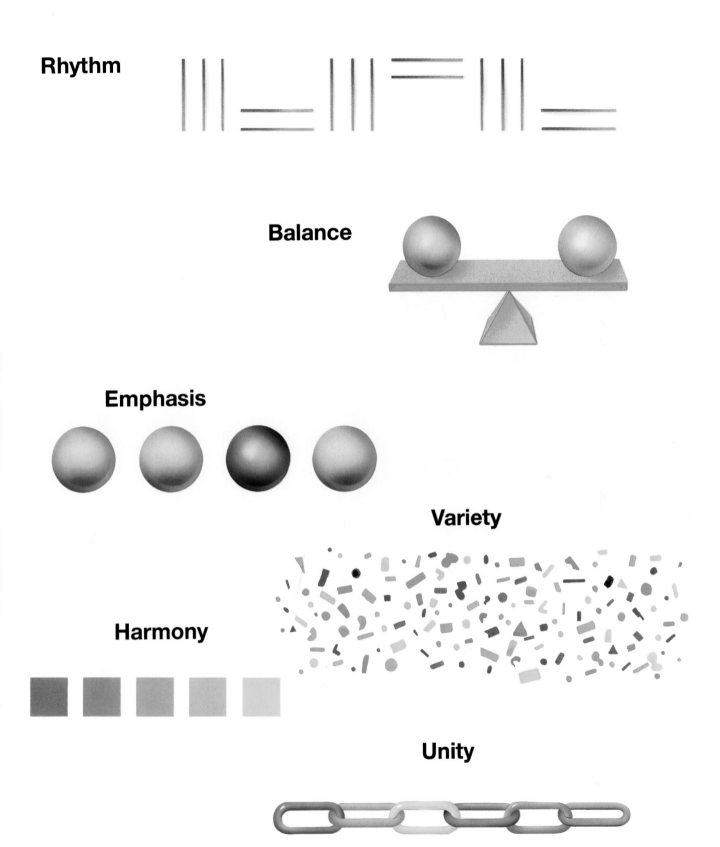

Every work of art has three parts.

They are

SUBJECT

The subject is the objects you can recognize.
If a work has no objects, the elements of art are the
subject.

COMPOSITION

The composition is how the elements and
principles are organized in the artwork.

CONTENT

The content is the message or meaning of the
artwork. When the work of art is functional, then the
function of the work is the meaning.

Philip Evergood. (American).
Her World. 1948. Oil on canvas.
48 x 35$\frac{5}{8}$ inches. Metropolitan
Museum of Art, New York.

Wassily Kandinsky. (Russian).
Improvisation #27. 1912. Oil on canvas.
47$\frac{3}{8}$ x 55$\frac{1}{4}$ inches. Metropolitan
Museum of Art, New York, The Alfred
Stieglitz Collection, 1949.

Michelangelo. (Italian).
David. (Detail). 1501–1504. Marble.
Galleria dell' Accademia, Florence, Italy.
Scala, Art Resource, New York.

Artist unknown. Teton, Lakota,
(American). *Parasol.* Buckskin, quilled
and beaded decoration. $25\frac{1}{2}$ x 23
inches. Courtesy of the Smithsonian
National Museum of the American
Indian, New York. George H.
Bingenheimer Collection. Photo by
David Heald.

In which work of art do you think the subject matter is very important?

In which artwork do you think composition is most important?

Which work seems to have the strongest message? Explain?

Which artwork's meaning relates to its function?

An Introduction to
Line and Shape

Artists use line and shape to create all kinds of art.

Pablo Picasso. (Spanish).
Mother and Child. 1922.
Oil on canvas. 100 × 81 cm.
The Baltimore Museum of
Art: The Cone Collection
formed by Dr. Claribel Cone
and Miss Etta Cone of
Baltimore, Maryland.
© 1998 Estate of Pablo
Picasso/Artist Rights
Society (ARS), New York.

Artists use a variety of lines to outline objects and show details.

- Which lines outline the objects in *Mother and Child?*
- How do lines show detail in the mother's hair? Where else do you see lines that show detail?

Artists also use geometric and free-form shapes.

- What main shape did Picasso use to draw the mother and child? What kind of shapes are the leaves?
- What complex geometric shape did Picasso use for the child's right foot?

Artist **P**rofile

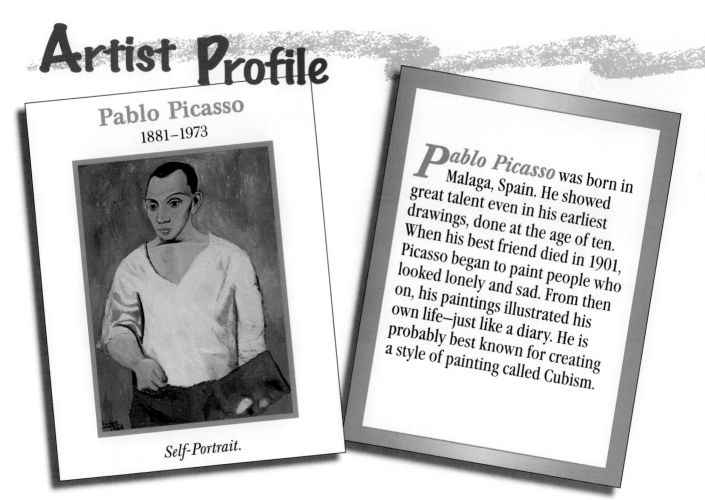

Pablo Picasso
1881–1973

Self-Portrait.

Pablo Picasso was born in Malaga, Spain. He showed great talent even in his earliest drawings, done at the age of ten. When his best friend died in 1901, Picasso began to paint people who looked lonely and sad. From then on, his paintings illustrated his own life—just like a diary. He is probably best known for creating a style of painting called Cubism.

Pablo Picasso and other artists use line and shape to help them create art. In this unit you will learn to use different kinds of lines. You will also learn how shapes are seen in everything around you. You will study:

- Kinds of Lines
- Line Variations
- Geometric and Free-Form Shapes

Lines and What They Express

Artists use different kinds of lines to create a mood or feeling in a painting or drawing.

Charles Burchfield. (American). *Orion in December.*
1959. Watercolor and pencil on paper.
$39\frac{7}{8} \times 32\frac{7}{8}$ inches. National Museum of American
Art, Washington, DC, Art Resource, NY.

Look at the two landscape paintings on these pages. *Orion in December* was painted by Charles Burchfield. *Bridge over a Pool of Water Lilies* was painted by Claude Monet about sixty years earlier. Both artists have used lines to express a mood felt in nature. Compare the moods of the two paintings.

Claude Monet. (French). *Bridge over a Pool of Water Lilies.*
1899. Oil on canvas. $36\frac{1}{2} \times 29$ inches. Metropolitan
Museum of Art, New York, New York.

Study both landscape paintings.

- ☑ Find the vertical lines.
- ☑ Find the horizontal lines.
- ☑ Identify the diagonal lines.
- ☑ Where are the curved lines in each painting?
- ☑ Find the lines that zigzag.

SEEING LIKE AN ARTIST

Look outside your classroom. Look for things such as trees, leaves, and grass. Find lines like the ones you found in the landscape paintings.

Using Lines

Lines are marks drawn by a tool such as a pencil, pen, or paintbrush as it moves across a surface. There are five different kinds of lines. Each one can make you feel a certain way.

 Vertical lines move straight up and down. They make things look tall, steady, and calm.

 Horizontal lines move straight across from side to side. They give a feeling of calm or peace.

 Diagonal lines are slanted. They look as if they are falling over or getting up. They make things look active.

 **Zigzag** lines are diagonal lines that connect. They give a feeling of excitement.

 **Curved** lines bend and change direction slowly. They give a feeling of graceful movement.

Practice

Use different kinds of lines to create a weather chart. Use white paper and markers.

1. Fold a sheet of paper into six equal boxes. Each box will show a different weather condition that occurs in nature—strong wind, rainstorm, and blizzard. Write the name of one of the weather conditions at the bottom of each box.

2. Use different kinds of lines like the ones above to draw the weather condition written at the bottom of each box.

Decide When you look at each box, does it show the feeling of the weather condition? How can you change the lines to improve them?

Anna Boynton. Age 8. *Twister.* Markers.

How does this student artist's weather scene make you feel?

Create

How do different kinds of weather make you feel? Draw a weather scene that causes you to have a certain feeling.

1. Think about the different kinds of weather where you live. What mood does each create?

2. Select the type of weather condition you would like to draw. Make a rough sketch to plan the scene. Experiment with different kinds of lines. Decide which lines will best express the mood you wish to create.

3. Draw your scene. Be sure to use the right kinds of lines to create a calm or active feeling.

Describe Name the different kinds of lines you used in your drawing.

Analyze Is the scene calm or active? How do the lines show this feeling?

Interpret If you were to change the lines, how would the mood or feeling be different?

Decide Did you successfully use lines to show a calm or active scene? If you could do this drawing over again, how would you change it?

Line Variation

Artists can change lines in a variety of ways to make their artwork more interesting.

Wassily Kandinsky. (Russian). *Improvisation No. 27.* 1912. Oil paint. $47\frac{3}{8} \times 55\frac{1}{4}$ inches. Metropolitan Museum of Art, New York, New York.

Look at the two paintings on these pages. *Improvisation No. 27* is a nonobjective painting by Wassily Kandinsky. Wang Chao's scroll painting was created around 400 years earlier. Even though both artists used lines, both paintings are very different. Wang used line to describe people and objects. Kandinsky used line as part of the subject.

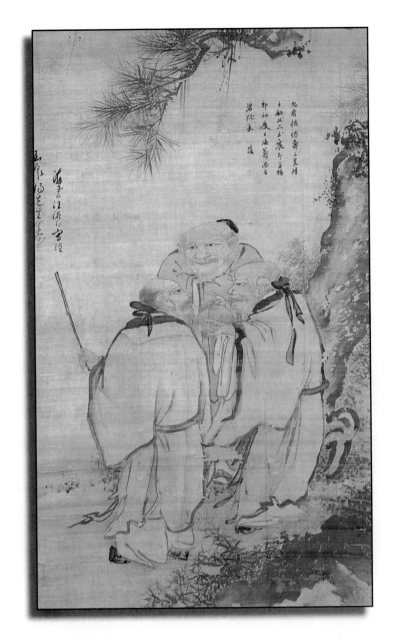

Wang Chao. (Chinese). *The Three Stars of Happiness, Wealth, and Longevity.* c. 1500. Hanging scroll. Ink and light colors on silk. $62\frac{1}{2} \times 37\frac{1}{2}$ inches. Courtesy of the Kimbell Art Museum, Fort Worth, Texas.

Study both paintings to find a variety of different lines.

✓ Find lines that are long and lines that are short.

✓ Find lines that are thick and lines that are thin.

✓ Do you see any lines that look rough? Where are they? Find the lines that look smooth.

✓ Where do you see lines that move in different directions?

SEEING LIKE AN ARTIST

Look around your classroom. Find lines like the ones you saw in the paintings.

Lesson 2

Using a Variety of Lines

Artists can change lines in many ways to make them look different. You saw **line variety** in the two paintings on the previous pages.

Lines can be **long** or **short**.

Lines can be **thick** or **thin**.

Lines can be **rough** or **smooth**.

Lines can be **broken** or **solid**.

Practice

Draw a variety of lines. Use white paper and crayons.

1. Use crayon to make as many different kinds of lines as you can on a sheet of paper.

2. Now use your crayon in different ways to make rough, smooth, thick, and thin lines.

Decide Have you filled your page with a variety of lines? Did you use your crayon in different ways to change how the lines look?

Heather Byrnes. Age 8. *On the Farm.* Watercolors.

What are the different types of lines this student artist used in her landscape?

Create

What does your favorite outdoor place look like? Draw it using a variety of lines.

1. Think about your favorite place. Is it the beach? A lake? A park? A farm? The mountains? What objects would you find there?

2. Using different kinds of lines, make several sketches of the objects you want to include in your landscape.

3. Use watercolor paints to create the landscape. Use large and small brushes to make many different kinds of lines.

Describe Describe the objects you included in your landscape painting.

Analyze List the different kinds of lines you used in your painting.

Interpret How do the lines you used affect the mood or feeling of your painting?

Decide Did you successfully use a variety of lines to paint the objects in your landscape?

Shapes

Artists use lines to create shapes.

Rachel Ruysch.
(Dutch). *Roses,
Convolvulus, Poppies
and Other Flowers in an
Urn on a Stone Ledge.*
c. 1745. Oil on canvas.
$42\frac{1}{2} \times 33$ inches. The
National Museum of
Women in the Arts,
Washington, DC,
Gift of Wallace and
Wilhelmina Holladay.

Look at the paintings on these pages. Rachel Ruysch
created her painting about flowers around
1745. *Arcanum* was painted by artist Janet Fish more
than 200 years later! Both artists have used lines to
create the shapes in their paintings.

Janet Fish. (American). *Arcanum.* 1990. Oil on canvas. 80 × 50 inches. Courtesy Janet Fish and D.C. Moore Gallery, New York, New York.

Study both still-life paintings to find the following shapes.

- Find as many round shapes as you can.
- Find the square shapes.
- Where are the triangles?
- Are there any oval shapes? Where?
- Locate the free-form shapes.

SEEING LIKE AN ARTIST
Think about or look outside and find different shapes found in your environment.

Using Shapes

Everything has a **shape**. They are flat, two-dimensional areas that are either geometric or free-form.

Here are some simple **geometric** shapes.

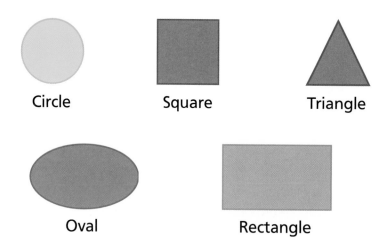

Circle   Square   Triangle

Oval   Rectangle

Free-form shapes are uneven and are not regular. They can look many different ways:

Lines can be used to outline all these shapes.

Practice

Outline geometric and free-form shapes.

1. Find three geometric and three free-form shapes in your classroom.

2. In the air, use your index finger to trace the outline of each object. Close one eye as you trace.

Decide Did you notice how the tip of your finger made a line in the air when you traced the outline of each object?

Kitzia Medina. Age 8. *Still Life.* Watercolors and oil pastels.

What geometric shapes do you see in this student artist's still life?

Create

What are some of the shapes you see in the objects around you? Paint a still-life picture using lines to make shapes.

1. Arrange five objects of different shapes and sizes in a variety of ways. Select the best arrangement.

2. Which object captures your attention most? Outline the shape of that object on your paper. In the same way, add the shapes of the other objects.

3. Begin to fill your shapes with different colors. Use one color at a time in several places on your picture. Continue to do this until your paper is filled with color.

Describe What geometric shapes did you use in your painting? What free-form shapes did you use in your painting?

Analyze What types of lines did you use to create the shapes?

Interpret Look at the first object you drew on your paper. Why did you decide to draw that object?

Decide If you could redo your painting, what would you do differently?

Complex Geometric Shapes

Artists use complex geometric shapes to create designs.

Look at the artwork on these pages. The double saddlebag was created in North America by a member of the Sioux Indians in 1880. The Mihrab (the focal area in an Islamic house of worship) was created in Iran about 500 years earlier, and is decorated with colorful tiles. Both pieces are decorated with complex geometric shapes.

Artist unknown. Sioux (United States). *Double Saddlebag.* 1875. Buckskin, canvas, glass beads, sinew, and wool. 113.7 × 33 cm. Detroit Institute of Arts, Detroit, Michigan.

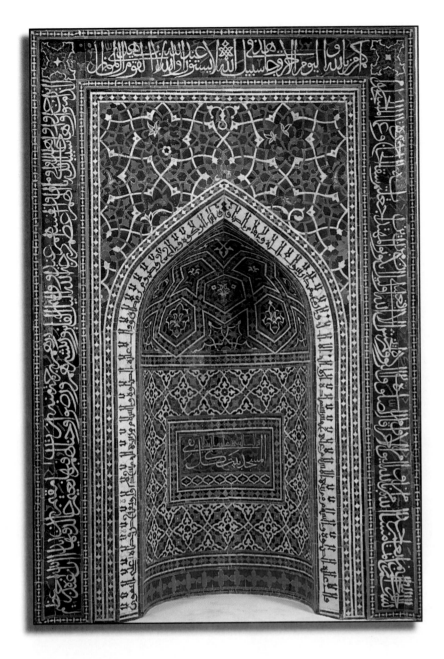

Artist unknown. (Iran). *Mihrab.*
1354. Faience mosaic of glazed
terra-cotta cut and embedded in
plaster. 11 feet 3 inches × 7 feet
6 inches. Metropolitan Museum of
Art, New York, New York.

Study both artworks and find the following
complex geometric shapes.

☑ Find the shapes that have six sides.

☑ Point to the large diamond shapes in the
saddlebag. Look closely to find smaller diamond
shapes in the Mihrab.

☑ Where do you see some star shapes?

☑ Look at the large shapes in the saddlebag. What
simple geometric shapes are used to make them?

SEEING LIKE
AN ARTIST
Look at the clothes
your classmates are
wearing. Are any of
them decorated with
shapes like the ones
you just found in the
artwork?

Using Complex Geometric Shapes

Complex geometric shapes are made by combining simple geometric shapes such as triangles, squares, and rectangles. You found examples of complex geometric shapes in the two artworks on the previous pages.

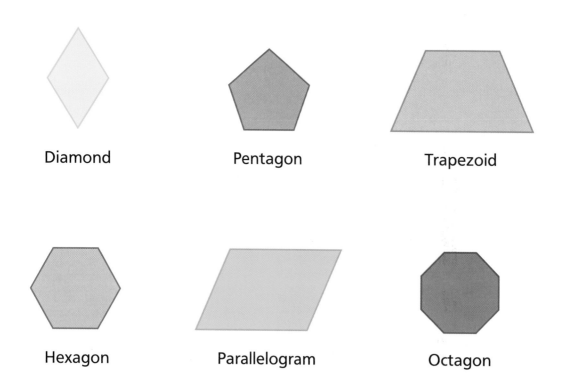

Diamond   Pentagon   Trapezoid

Hexagon   Parallelogram   Octagon

Practice

Draw simple geometric shapes to create complex geometric shapes. Use pencil.

1. Fold a sheet of paper into six equal boxes. Print the name of a complex geometric shape at the bottom of each box.

2. Draw one complex geometric shape in each box.

Decide Find the simple shapes in each complex geometric shape.

Name the geometric shapes in this student artist's robot.

Ashley Quick. Age 8. *Crazy Robot.*
Colored construction paper.

Create

How can you use geometric shapes to create a design? Design a robot using geometric shapes.

1. Imagine a robot you can create with complex geometric shapes.

2. Use your imagination to design a robot using simple and complex geometric shapes.

3. Use your scrap pieces of paper to design a frame or border for your collage.

Describe Describe the robot you created.

Analyze Name the simple and complex geometric shapes you used.

Interpret Give your robot a name.

Decide If you could create this robot again, what would you do differently?

Shapes in Architecture

**Architects use geometric and free-form
shapes to design buildings.**

Berenice Abbott. (American). *Nos. 4, 6, & 8 Fifth Avenue.* 1936.
Black-and-white photograph. Museum of the City of New York,
neg. 87, New York, New York.

Look at the artwork on these pages. Each one
includes an image of buildings. *Nos. 4, 6, & 8
Fifth Avenue* is a photograph of three private homes
in New York. It was taken by Berenice Abbott in 1936.
At about the same time, artist Joseph Henry Sharp
painted *Sunset Dance-Ceremony to the Evening Sun.*
Both works of art show how geometric and free-form
shapes are used in architecture.

Joseph Henry Sharp. (American). *Sunset Dance-Ceremony to the Evening Sun.* 1924. Oil on canvas. $25\frac{1}{8} \times 30$ inches. National Museum of American Art, Washington, DC/Art Resource, NY.

Study the buildings in both pieces of artwork to find the following shapes.

- ✓ Point to all the square shapes you see.
- ✓ Where are the rectangles?
- ✓ Find the triangles.
- ✓ Do you see any circles? Where are they?
- ✓ Find some free-form shapes.

SEEING LIKE AN ARTIST

Go outside your classroom and look at the buildings in the neighborhood. Look for geometric and free-form shapes.

Shapes in Architecture

Architecture is the art of designing and planning buildings for people. You saw examples of architecture in the artwork on the previous pages. An **architect** is the person or artist who plans and designs buildings. Architects use **geometric** and **free-form shapes** in their designs.

Roofs	Windows	Doors

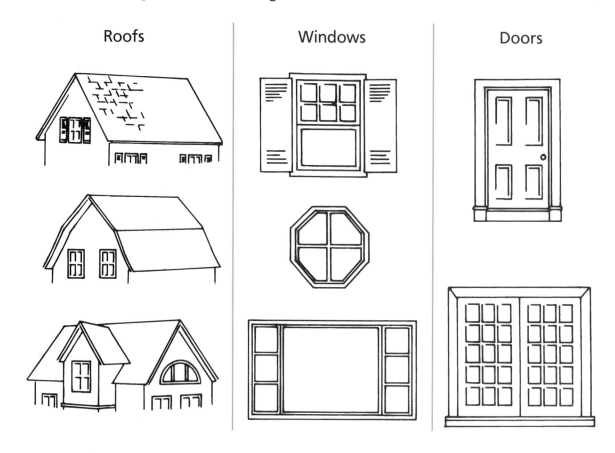

Practice

Illustrate geometric and free-form shapes in architecture. Use pencil.

1. On a sheet of paper, use your pencil to draw a large geometric shape to create the outline of a house or building.

2. Use your imagination to add smaller geometric and free-form shapes to create the roof, windows, and doors.

Decide Is your drawing of a building or house where people live or work? Does it have different kinds of shapes?

Edwin Vasquez. Age 8. *My School.* Marker

Which parts of this student artist's drawing are examples of free-form and which are geometric shapes?

Create

In the world around you, what buildings are designed with geometric and free-form shapes? Draw a building using geometric and free-form shapes.

1. Walk outside and choose an area of your school building that you would like to draw.

2. Point out all the geometric shapes you see. Now look for the free-form shapes.

3. Draw the area of your school building you selected. Make sure you include all the geometric and free-form shapes you see.

Describe List the simple and complex geometric shapes you used in your drawing. Describe the free-form shapes you used.

Analyze Which shape is used most?

Interpret How could you completely change the appearance of the building with different shapes?

Decide Does your drawing look like your school building? If not, what needs to be changed to improve your drawing?

Shapes All Around Us

Artists use geometric and free-form shapes in portraits.

John Singleton Copley. (American). *Daniel Crommelin Verplanck.* 1771. Oil on canvas. $49\frac{1}{2} \times 40$ inches. Metropolitan Museum of Art, New York, New York.

A portrait is a picture of a person. Look at the portraits on these two pages. *Daniel Crommelin Verplanck* was painted by John Singleton Copley in 1771. About 150 years later, Allen E. Cole used a camera to take the photograph of *Silas Johnson.* Both portraits show geometric and free-form shapes.

Allen E. Cole. (American). *Silas Johnson*. 1920s. Hand-tinted photograph. Western Reserve Historical Society, Cleveland, Ohio.

Study both portraits to find the following geometric and free-form shapes.

- Find the circles.
- Point to the rectangles you see.
- Are there any triangles?
- Find the free-form shapes.
- Where are the oval shapes?

Using Shapes

Shapes are all around us. You have already seen different shapes in the portraits on pages 36 and 37.

Free-form shapes can be found in nature. Puddles, clouds, and flowers are examples of free-form shapes found in nature. People are free-form shapes.

Geometric shapes are usually found in objects that are made by people. Buildings, furniture, and road signs are some examples.

Most objects have one main shape. Some objects are made of many smaller shapes.

Practice

Draw the shapes of an object. Use pencil.

1. Choose an object from your classroom to draw. Find the smaller geometric or free-form shapes that make it.

2. On a sheet of paper, draw the object by putting together the smaller shapes you see.

Decide Does your drawing have the same shape as the actual object? Did you draw the smaller shapes that make it up?

What geometric shape is the face in this student artist's portrait?

Carolina Monsure. Age 8. *Self-Portrait*. Oil pastel.

Create

What are the shapes of the faces of some of the people you know? Draw a portrait using geometric and free-form shapes.

1. Ask a classmate to be your model. Select some objects from the classroom to use as props. Have your model use some of these props as they pose for you.

2. Look very carefully at your model. Find the geometric and free-form shapes.

3. Use chalk to draw your model and the props. Use lines to create all the geometric and free-form shapes you see. Fill the shapes with oil pastels.

Describe Identify the shapes you used in your portrait.

Analyze Where did you use the geometric shapes? Where did you use free-form shapes?

Interpret Give your portrait a title. Then, invite your model to give the portrait a title.

Decide Did your portrait turn out as you had hoped? Why or why not? If you were able to do this artwork over again, what would you do to improve it?

Lines and Shapes in Dance

American Indian Dance Theatre:
Zuni, *"Eagle Dance."*

The eagle is an important symbol for Native Americans. It stands for someone who is strong and wise. Native Americans perform an Eagle Dance. The dancers try to copy the eagle's movements. The dancers' bodies form different shapes and create straight, diagonal, and curved lines.

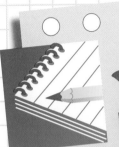

What To Do

Create an original eagle dance.

Materials
✓ pictures of eagles in different positions

1. Study the pictures carefully. Then, list everything you know about the eagle.

2. Look closely at the pictures. Try showing their positions with your body.

3. Make a list of actions done by the eagle. Pick one action. Explore how you can show the action with movements of your body.

4. Create a simple dance about the eagle. First, use your body to show three different positions of the eagle. Next, select one or two actions. Do each action for eight counts. End in a "perched" eagle shape.

5. Perform your dance in a group.

Describe Describe the way you made your three eagle shapes.

Analyze Explain how you made your eagle movements to show actions.

Interpret How does your dance express the spirit and strength of the eagle?

Decide How well did you show what an eagle is like? How did you use shape and line?

Extra Credit • • • • • • • • • • • •

Work with a partner. One of you can play a steady beat on a drum. The other can perform the eagle dance.

Dance

Line and Shape

Reviewing Main Ideas

The lessons and activities in this unit cover different kinds of lines and shapes that artists use in works of art.

1. **Lines** are made when a tool such as a pencil moves across a surface. There are five different kinds of lines. Each one expresses a different feeling.

   - **Vertical** lines make things look tall and calm.

   - **Horizontal** lines give a feeling of calm or peace.

   - **Diagonal** lines make objects seem unsteady.

   - **Zigzag** lines cause a feeling of excitement.

   - **Curved** lines give a feeling of graceful movement.

2. **Line variations** make lines look different. (short or long, thick or thin, rough or smooth, or broken or solid)

3. **Shapes** are flat, two-dimensional areas. There are two types of shapes.

   - Circles, squares, triangles, ovals, and rectangles are *simple geometric shapes.*

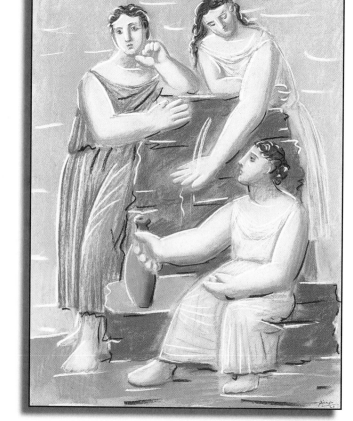

Pablo Picasso. (Spanish). *Three Women at the Fountain.* 1921. Pastel on blue paper. 25 × 19$\frac{1}{8}$ inches. Museum of Fine Arts, Houston, TX; Gift of Miss Ima Hogg and other Trustees of the Varner-Bayou Bend Heritage Fund.

- **Free-form shapes** are uneven and not regular. People are free-form shapes.
4. **Complex geometric shapes** are made by combining simple geometric shapes. (diamond, pentagon, hexagon, octagon, trapezoid, and parallelogram)
5. **Architecture** is the art of designing and planning buildings. An *architect* is the person who does the planning and designing.

Summing Up

Look at the painting by Picasso. Notice how he used the different lines and shapes you learned about in this unit.

- Find at least three different kinds of lines. What feeling does each express?
- Find two different line variations.
- Where do you see simple and complex geometric shapes?

Line and shape are important elements in drawings, paintings, and prints. By using lines and shapes, artists can describe to others the objects, areas, and details they see.

Careers in Art
Art Educator

Kathy Perales is an art educator. Art educators teach people all about art. They show students how to look at and talk about artworks. They also teach them how to produce their own artwork. Perales lives in Canyon Lake, Texas. She thinks the best part of being an art educator is being able to help students improve their skills. Their excitement as they discover success makes all her hard work worth it. Perales studied art at college to get ready for her exciting career.

Kathy Perales, Art Educator

An Introduction to
Color and Value

Artists use color and value to make their artwork special.

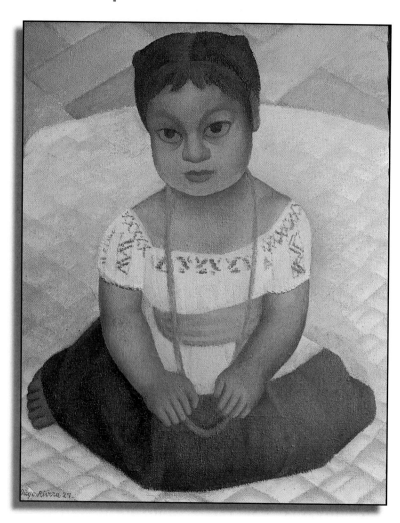

Diego Rivera. (Mexican).
Kneeling Child on Yellow Background.
1927. Oil on canvas. $25\frac{1}{2} \times 21$ inches.
San Francisco Museum of Modern
Art, San Francisco, California.
Bequest of Elise S. Haas. Photo by
Ben Blackwell.

Artists use **color** to create a certain feeling or emotion in a work of art.

- What colors do you see in *Kneeling Child on Yellow Background?*
- How do the colors make you feel?

Some artists use different **values** of a color to show the highlights and shadows of an object.

- Where did Rivera use light and dark color values on the young girl's face?
- Where else do you see light and dark values of a color?

Artist Profile

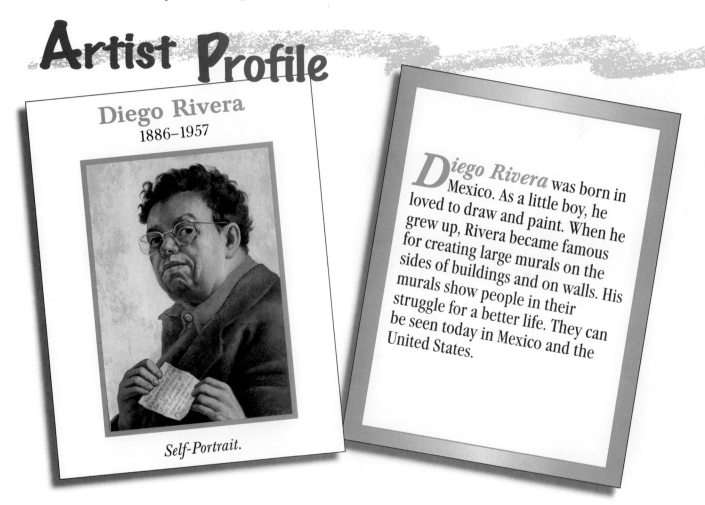

Diego Rivera
1886–1957

Self-Portrait.

Diego Rivera was born in Mexico. As a little boy, he loved to draw and paint. When he grew up, Rivera became famous for creating large murals on the sides of buildings and on walls. His murals show people in their struggle for a better life. They can be seen today in Mexico and the United States.

Diego Rivera and other artists use color and value to help them create art. In this unit you will learn about colors and the feelings they create. You will practice mixing and using colors. You will study:

- Primary and Secondary Colors
- Value
- Intermediate Colors
- Color Wheel
- Warm and Cool Colors
- Color Contrast

Looking at Color

Artists mix three primary colors to create many other colors. Color can express different feelings or moods in art.

Shirley Ximena Hopper Russell. (American). *Boys' Day.* 1935. Oil on canvas. $29\frac{5}{8} \times 24\frac{5}{8}$ inches. Honolulu Academy of Arts. Honolulu, Hawaii, Gift of Henry B. Clark, Jr.

Shirley Russell's painting *Boys' Day* is about a holiday celebrated by people flying flags and colorful streamers. Faith Ringgold created the story quilt *Tar Beach.* It tells the story of a third grader who imagines herself flying high above the rooftops of New York. Both artists use color to show the mood of the events they painted.

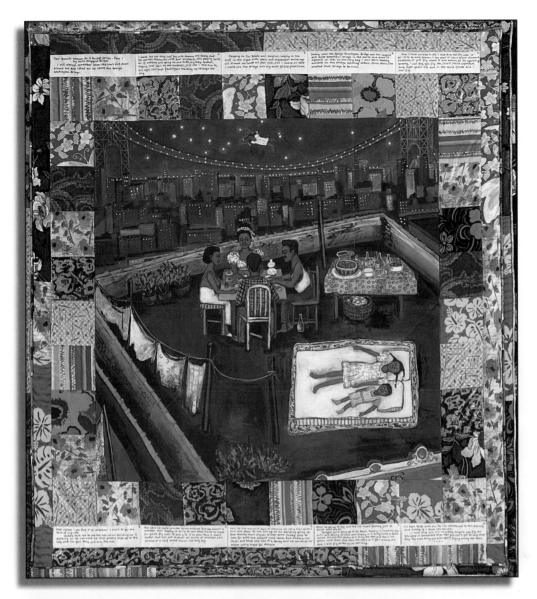

Faith Ringgold. (American). *Tar Beach.* 1988. Acrylic on canvas bordered with printed, painted, quilted, and pieced cloth. $74\frac{5}{8} \times 68\frac{1}{2}$ inches. © 1988 Faith Ringgold Inc. Solomon R. Guggenheim Museum, New York, New York. Photograph by David Heald © The Solomon R. Guggenheim Foundation, New York.

Study both paintings to find the following colors.

- ✓ Find the primary colors—red, yellow, and blue.

- ✓ Point to the secondary colors—orange, green, and violet.

- ✓ Where are the light colors? The dark colors?

SEEING LIKE AN ARTIST

Look in a magazine or an advertisement. Find the same colors that you saw in the paintings.

Using Colors

Colors are used to express different moods or feelings in works of art. **Hue** is another name for color. The three **primary colors** are red, yellow, and blue. They cannot be made by mixing other colors.

The **secondary colors** are made by mixing two primary colors together.

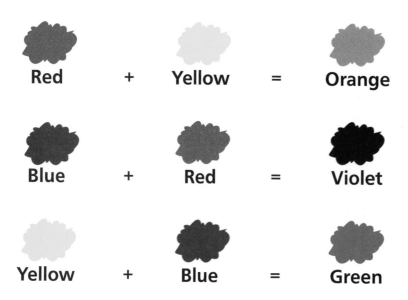

Red	+	Yellow	=	Orange
Blue	+	Red	=	Violet
Yellow	+	Blue	=	Green

Value is the lightness or darkness of a color. Adding white makes a color lighter. Adding black makes a color darker. When the value of a color is lighter, it is called a **tint**. When the value of a color is darker, it is called a **shade**.

Practice

Hold a "Color Bee."

1. Divide into four teams. Think up color questions based on the above information.

2. Write each question on a piece of paper. Fold the papers and put them into a question box.

3. Take turns pulling questions from the box and answering them.

Decide Did each team write questions? Were the questions based on colors and value? Were the teams able to answer the questions?

Domenique Chery. Age 8. *The Market Place.* Mixed-media.

What mood does this student artist create
in her artwork?

Create

**What colors do you like? Draw a picture of
a special event using the colors that show
the feeling of that event.**

1. Think of ways that you, your family, and
   friends celebrate special events. Choose
   one for your drawing. What objects do you
   need to include? What colors will you use
   to show the mood of this event?

2. Draw the event or occasion with colored
   markers on white construction paper.

3. Fill your paper with color.

Describe What special event
did you draw? Describe the
people and objects. Point to
the tints and shades.

Analyze Name the colors you
used. Did you use some colors
for special effects?

Interpret What is the mood of
your event?

Decide If you could do this
drawing again, how would you
improve it?

Intermediate Colors

Some artists use intermediate colors in their work
to express different ideas and emotions.

Artist unknown. (Peru). **Hat: Birds and Geometric Patterns.** 700–1000.
Alpaca and cotton. $4\frac{1}{2} \times 5$ inches. The Seattle Art Museum, Gift of Jack Lenor Larson.
Photo by Paul Macapia Seattle, Washington.

Look at the two works of art on these pages. The cap was woven in the South American country now named Peru, sometime between A.D. 700 and 1000. William Wiley's painting was done in the United States almost 1000 years later. Both artists used intermediate colors in their works.

William T. Wiley. (American). *Remedial Archaeology and the Like.* 1986. Acrylic and graphite on canvas. 100 × 165 inches. Collection of the Birmingham Museum of Art, Birmingham, Alabama; Museum purchase with funds provided by the National Endowment for the Arts and Museum Store.

S**tudy** both artworks to find the intermediate colors.

✓ Find the yellow-orange hues. Where are the red-orange hues?

✓ What other intermediate colors can you find?

SEEING LIKE AN ARTIST
Look through this unit. Find more examples of the colors you saw in the art on these pages.

Using Intermediate Colors

Intermediate colors are made by mixing a primary color and a secondary color. There are six intermediate colors—red-orange, yellow-orange, yellow-green, blue-green, blue-violet, and red-violet.

A color wheel is an artist's way of organizing these 12 colors.

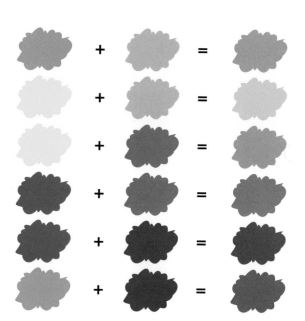

Practice

Find intermediate colors. Use magazines and scissors.

1. Fold a sheet of paper into six equal boxes. Write the name of one intermediate color in each box.

2. Find examples of intermediate colors in magazines. Glue each example into the correct box.

Decide Did you find all six intermediate colors?

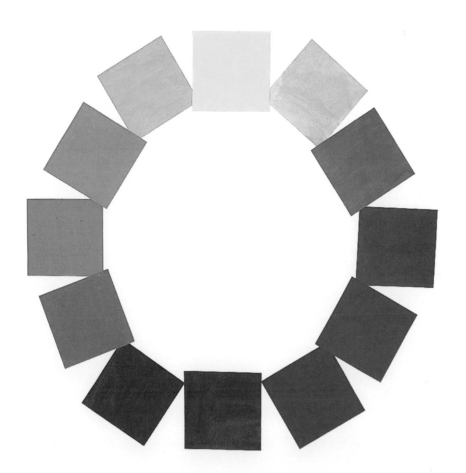

Which colors make you happy? Which colors make you sad?

Ivie Gulbrandson and others. Age 8. *A Color Wheel.* Tempera.

Create

What colors make you feel happy? Sad? Excited? Create a giant color wheel using primary, secondary, and intermediate colors.

1. Cut a large sheet of drawing paper into 12 pieces. Put a large spoonful of red, yellow, and blue paint on a paper plate. Paint three pieces of paper with primary colors. Mix secondary colors and paint three more pieces of paper.

2. Now mix the intermediate colors. Paint the six remaining pieces of paper with these colors.

3. Use your color samples to make a giant temporary class color wheel on the floor.

Describe Name the primary, secondary, and intermediate colors in the color wheel.

Analyze Compare the intermediate colors in the color wheel. Why do you think some look different?

Interpret How do each of the intermediate colors make you feel?

Decide Which of the intermediate colors came out best? Which would you redo? Why?

Lesson 2

Color Wheel

Artists use the color wheel to get information and ideas about spectral and intermediate colors and how they relate to one another.

Man Ray. (American). *La Fortune*. 1938. Oil on canvas. 24 × 29 inches. © Collection of the Whitney Museum of American Art, New York, New York. © 1998 Artists Rights Society (ARS), New York/ADAGP/Man Ray Trust, Paris.

Look at the works of art on these pages. Both artists have used spectral colors. *La Fortune* was painted by Man Ray in 1938. At about the same time, Calvin Jones created *Brilliant as the Sun upon the World.*

Calvin Jones. (American). *Brilliant as the Sun Upon the World.*

Study both works of art to find the following colors.

- ✓ Find the primary colors.
- ✓ Where are the secondary colors?
- ✓ Which artist used intermediate colors?

SEEING LIKE AN ARTIST

Look around you to see how many colors of the spectrum you can find.

Using a Color Wheel

The range of colors that comes from light is called the **color spectrum**. Rainbows are the most famous display of this spectrum in nature. The spectrum that artists use is bent into the shape of a circle. It is called a **color wheel**.

The color wheel includes the six spectral colors and six intermediate colors. Like the colors in the spectrum, these colors are always placed in the same order, no matter which way you turn the wheel.

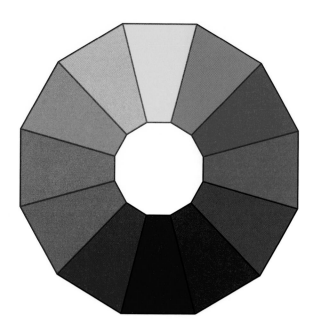

Practice

Make a color chart. Use crayons.

1. Divide paper in half. Label one side "Spectral Colors" and other side "Intermediate Colors."

2. Use crayons to show the colors in order on each side.

Decide Name the spectral and intermediate colors in their correct order.

Michael Dean. Age 8. Tempera.

Name this student artist's color wheel amusement ride.

Create

What is your favorite amusement ride? Create an amusement ride for the Rainbow Park using the colors of a color wheel.

1. Think about an amusement ride you can make using all the colors from a color wheel in order.

2. Be creative. Just remember that the colors have to follow the order of the color wheel.

Describe Name all the colors you used in your ride?

Analyze How did you organize your colors?

Interpret Give your ride a name.

Decide Did you make an interesting ride?

Lesson 3

Cool Colors

Artists use cool colors to suggest a calm emotion or feeling. Cool colors often remind people of cool things such as ice, snow, water, or grass.

Yves Tanguy. (French). *Indefinite Divisibility.* 1942. Oil on canvas. 40 × 35 inches. Albright Knox Art Gallery, Buffalo, New York, Room of Contemporary Art Fund, 1945 © 1998 Artists Rights Society (ARS) New York/ADAGP, Paris.

Look at the artwork on these pages. The title of Tanguy's painting is almost a brainteaser. It says the subject of the painting can be divided over and over. Emily Carr turns her sky into a roller coaster. Both artists use cool colors in their art.

Emily Carr. (Canadian). *Sky.* 1935. Oil on woven paper. 58.7 × 90.7 cm. National Gallery of Canada. Ottawa, Canada.

Study both works of art to find the following cool colors.

- ✓ Find the blues.

- ✓ Find the intermediate colors blue-green and blue-violet.

- ✓ How do the cool colors affect the mood of each painting?

Using Cool Colors

Blue, green, and violet are **cool colors**. They remind us of cool things such as grass, water, and ice. Yellow-green, green, blue-green, blue, violet, and blue-violet are cool colors that are related, like members of a family. You can find them on a color wheel to see what they have in common.

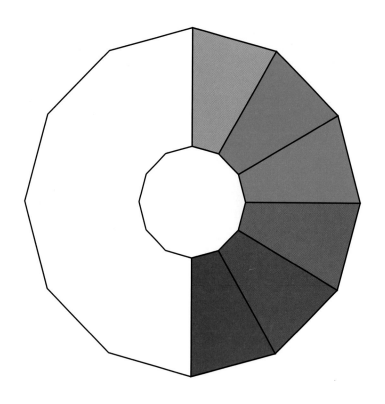

Practice

Create a drawing using cool colors. Use crayons and white paper.

1. Write these words on a sheet of paper: *ocean, sky, grapes, grass, leaves,* and *lettuce.*

2. On the same sheet of paper, create a drawing including each of the objects listed above. Using the correct cool colors, color the objects.

Decide Were you successful at using the cool colors to color your objects?

Give this student artist's sculpture a name that ties its cool colors with the environment.

Jenna Mooney. Age 8. *A Park in the Future.* Mixed-media.

Create

Where in your environment do you see cool colors? Design a sculpture of an environment using cool colors.

1. Think of ideas dealing with your environment, such as an animal habitat or a playground in the year 3001. Choose an idea and sketch a few things you would find there.

2. Select several pieces of cool-colored paper. Choose one piece for the base. Outline objects you want in your environment on the other sheets of paper and cut them out. Add detail with oil pastels in cool colors. Attach the objects to your base.

Describe Describe your environment. What cool colors did you use?

Analyze What objects did you use in your environment? How did you decide where to place them?

Interpret How did using only cool colors affect the mood of your environment?

Decide If you could redo your sculpture, what would you do? If you could add other colors, what would they be?

Warm Colors

Artists use warm colors to add warmth to a piece of artwork. Warm colors often remind people of the sun, fire, and light.

Paul Klee. (Swiss). *Rotes Haus.* 1929. Oil on canvas mounted on cardboard. $10 \times 10\frac{7}{8}$ inches. San Francisco Museum of Modern Art, San Francisco, California. Gift of the Ojerassi Art Trust.

Look at the artwork on these pages. *Rotes Haus* means "red house." *Firebirds* is a **batik** painting, which uses hot wax and colored dyes to create a design on fabric. Both artists have used warm colors in their artwork.

Rosalind Ragans. (American). *Firebirds.* 1983. Dye on cotton. 36 × 48 inches. Private collection.

Study both works of art to find the following warm colors.

✓ Find the spectral hues red, orange, and yellow.

✓ Where are the intermediate hues red-orange and yellow-orange?

✓ How would you describe the mood or feeling of each piece?

Using Warm Colors

Warm colors are the **spectral colors** yellow, orange, and red that give a feeling of warmth in a work of art. They can be found opposite the cool colors on the color wheel.

Red-violet, red, red-orange, orange, yellow-orange, and yellow are warm colors that are related. They remind many people of warm or hot things like fire and the sun.

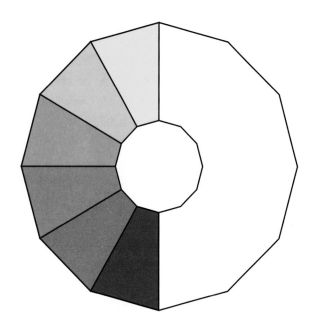

Practice

Mix a variety of warm colors. Use watercolor paints, brushes, and white paper.

1. Fold your paper into three equal parts. Paint the first box red, the middle box orange, and the last box yellow.

2. While the paint is still wet, add different amounts of violet to the red box, then mix.

3. In the same way, add and mix red to the orange, and orange to the yellow.

Decide Did you mix a variety of warm intermediate colors?

Michael Powell. Age 8. *The Dream.* Oil pastels and watercolor.

What makes this student artwork imaginary?

Create

What colors in your environment give you a feeling of warmth? Create an imaginative painting using warm colors.

1. Use your imagination to create a fantasy landscape that includes three unrelated items such as a matchstick, a bowling pin, and a pair of sunglasses. Make a rough sketch of your idea.

2. Use lines to draw your idea on a sheet of white paper with warm-colored oil pastels.

3. Mix a variety of warm values with watercolor paint. Paint your scene. Remember that the values will get lighter as you add more water to your paint.

Describe Name all the warm colors you used in your landscape.

Analyze What objects did you include in your imaginative painting?

Interpret How did using only warm colors affect the mood of your imaginative painting? If you added cool colors to your painting, how would the mood be different?

Decide If you could do this artwork over again, how would you improve it?

Color Contrast

Artists use contrast in artwork to make colors and subjects stand out.

Idelle Weber. (America). *Pistia Kew.* 1989. Oil on linen. 58 × 59 inches. Schmidt Bingham Gallery, New York, New York.

Look at the artwork on these pages. *Pistia Kew* was painted by Idelle Weber in 1989. The covered jar was created in China about 400 years ago. Both works show contrast of warm and cool colors.

Unit 2

Artist unknown. (China). *Covered Jar.* 1522–1566. Porcelain painted with underglaze cobalt blue and overglaze enamels. 18$\frac{1}{2}$ inches high, 15$\frac{3}{4}$ inches diameter. The Asia Society, New York, Mr. and Mrs. John D. Rockefeller 3rd Collection/Photo by Lynton Gardiner.

Study both works of art to find the contrast between warm and cool colors.

✓ Find all the cool colors. Are they placed near each other?

✓ Locate all the warm colors. Where are they placed?

✓ Which work has more warm colors?

✓ Find the colors that first catch your attention. Which colors are they?

SEEING LIKE AN ARTIST
Look around your classroom and find examples of cool colors that are near warm colors.

Using Color Contrast

Artists use **contrast** in order to show differences between two things.

The **warm colors** red, orange, and yellow come forward and attract your attention first. So do their related intermediate colors. The **cool colors** blue, green, and violet—and their related intermediate colors—seem to move away from you.

When warm colors are placed next to cool colors, a contrast is created.

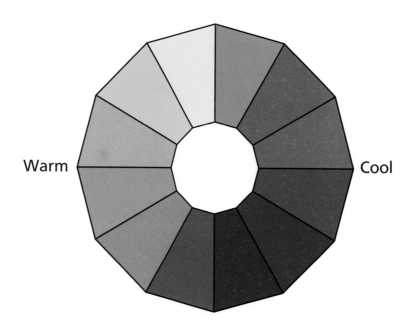

Warm   Cool

Practice

Illustrate color contrast. Use oil pastels and white paper.

1. On a sheet of paper, place cool colors next to warm colors.

2. Mix the intermediate colors by blending the primary and secondary colors. Fill your paper with color contrasts.

Decide Did you fill your paper with color contrasts? Are the warm colors next to the cool colors? Why do you see the warm colors first?

Laura Littlejohn. Age 8. Mixed-media.

How would the mood of this student artist's artwork change if the background contained warm colors and the creatures were made using cool colors?

Create

What objects in an underwater environment would you find that are warm-colored? Create a group mural contrasting warm and cool colors.

1. Think about the warm and cool colors you see underwater. In a small group, make a list of underwater creatures. Draw the creatures on sheets of warm-colored construction paper. Use warm-colored oil pastels to add color and detail. Cut out the shapes.

2. As a team, paint an underwater scene on a very large sheet of paper. Mix a variety of cool colors to create water and plant life.

3. When the paint is dry, arrange and glue the sea creatures in place.

Describe Describe the creatures your group created.

Analyze Which cool colors did you use in your mural? Which warm colors did you use in your mural?

Interpret How did the mood or feeling of your mural change when you added the warm-colored sea creatures to the cool background?

Decide If you could do this mural again, what would you do differently?

Color and Value in Storytelling

What kind of story might you tell to go with this picture?

dr. Jester Hairston is a grandson of slaves. He retells the stories that he heard and loved as a child. Hairston expresses the moods of a story by using his voice. He uses his voice as artists use colors and values. He makes his voice sound warm or cool. He speaks softly or deeply, in a high or low tone.

What To Do

Tell a folktale in a rap style.

Materials
✔ a tale or story
✔ paper and pencil

1. Read a folktale or a mystery.

2. Talk about the big idea of the story. Then, list what happened in the story in the correct order.

3. Practice telling the story. Use your voice to express feeling. A deep tone can express darkness. A high voice can express lightness. Speak softly or loudly, slowly or quickly, to match the mood of what's happening in the story.

4. Choose one phrase or sentence to sing as a chorus between parts of the story.

5. Take turns telling parts of the story. Sing the chorus together after each part.

Describe What are the different ways you used your voice to tell the story?

Analyze Explain what is different about telling a story in a rap style.

Interpret What moods did you create? How was your tone of voice like the values and colors in a painting?

Decide Did the chorus improve the storytelling? If not, what would you do differently?

Extra Credit · · · · · · · · · · · · · · ·

Make up your own story. Then, tell it in a rap style with a chorus. Perform it for others.

Color and Value

Reviewing Main Ideas

The lessons and activities in this unit cover color and value. These are used by artists to create certain moods or feelings in works of art.

1. **Primary colors** are pure colors. They are red, yellow, and blue.

2. **Secondary colors** are made by mixing two primary colors together. These are orange, green, and violet.

3. **Value** is the lightness or darkness of a color.

   • A **tint** is made by adding white to a color.

   • Adding black to a color creates a **shade.**

4. **Intermediate colors** are made by mixing a primary color and a secondary color. There are six intermediate colors.

5. The **color wheel** is a tool for organizing the twelve colors.

Andre Derain. (French). *The Turning Road, L'Estaque,* 1906. Oil on canvas. 51 × 76$\frac{3}{4}$ inches. Museum of Fine Arts, Houston, Texas. The John A. and Audrey Jones Beck Collection.

6. **Cool colors** are blue, green, and violet. They remind us of cool things. Yellow-green, blue-green, and blue-violet are cool colors that are *related*.

7. **Warm colors** are red, yellow, and orange. Red-violet. red-orange, and yellow-orange are warm colors that are related.

8. **Contrast** is used in order to show differences in two things, such as placing a warm color next to a cool color.

Summing Up

Look at the painting by Derain. Notice how he used value and a variety of colors covered in this unit.

- Find the primary and secondary colors.
- Name at least three different intermediate colors.
- Where do you see light and dark values in this landscape?
- Does Derain contrast warm and cool colors anywhere?

Color and value are important elements in paintings and drawings. By using certain colors and values, artists can express a particular feeling or emotion in an artwork.

Let's Visit a Museum

The Museum of Fine Arts in Houston, Texas, is the largest art museum in the Southwest. Its collection contains over 27,000 works of art. There you can see examples of styles of art from different periods in history. There is also a large collection of American decorative arts including furniture, paintings, metals, ceramics, glass, and textiles. If you visit the museum, you can walk in the museum's sculpture garden and see sculptures created by many nineteenth- and twentieth-century artists.

The Museum of Fine Arts, Houston

An Introduction to
Space and Form

Artists use space and form to make all kinds of artwork.

Michelangelo (Italian). *David*. (Detail). 1501–1504. Marble. Galleria dell' Accademia, Florence, Italy. Scala, Art Resource, New York.

Artists create **space** in artworks that are two dimensional and three dimensional.

- Which parts of *David* are behind or partly covered by other parts?
- Describe the area around the sculpture.

Artists create **form** in three-dimensional artwork.

- Which areas of the sculpture are raised? Which parts appear to be farther back?
- If you walked around to the back of this sculpture, how do you think David's head would look on the other side?

Artist **P**rofile

Michelangelo
(1475–1564)

Self-Portrait.

Michelangelo was born in Caprese, Italy. When he was very young, he was cared for by a stonecutter's wife. He grew up carving and drawing. Michelangelo was a great sculptor, architect, painter, poet, and engineer. Although he loved sculpting, he is probably most famous for his huge painting on the ceiling of the Sistine Chapel in Rome, Italy.

In this unit you will learn about and practice techniques to create the appearance of space on a flat surface. You will also learn about three-dimensional forms. Here are the topics you will study:

- Space
- Depth
- Overlapping
- Form
- Sculpture

Positive and Negative Space

Artists use positive and negative space in their artwork.

Artist unknown. Coastal Inca (Peru). *Sleeveless Shirt (two cats)*. c. 1438–1532. Wool and cotton. Metropolitan Museum of Art, Nelson Rockefeller Collection, New York, New York.

Look at the artwork on these pages. *Sleeveless Shirt (two cats)* is an **appliqué**, or decoration made from cloth cutouts. The cotton cloth shapes were sewn onto a woolen background. *Tree of Life* is a paper cutout. Positive and negative spaces bring out the design in both works.

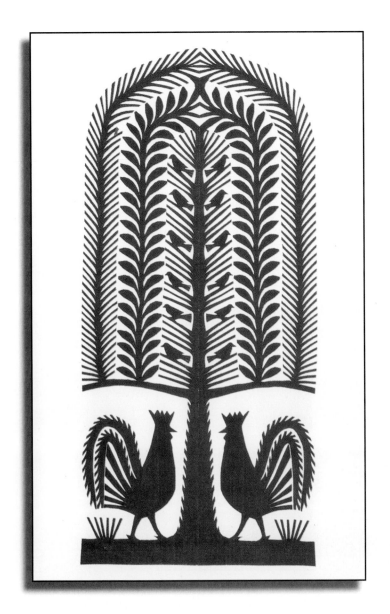

Stanistawa Bakula. (Polish).
Tree of Life. 1962. Cut paper.
$12\frac{3}{8} \times 7\frac{1}{2}$ inches. From the Girard
Foundation Collection, in the
Museum of International Folk Art,
a unit of the Museum of New
Mexico, Santa Fe, New Mexico.

Study both works of art to find examples of
positive and negative space.

- What objects do you see in each work? What colors
  are they?

- What colors are the negative spaces around the
  objects in each work?

- How do the empty spaces in both artworks help
  make the objects stand out?

SEEING LIKE
AN ARTIST
Notice the shapes of
clouds. What shapes
do you see in the
spaces around them?

Using Positive and Negative Space

In a work of art, the area that shapes and objects fill is called **positive space**. The empty area around them is called **negative space**.

Negative space can be just as important as positive space. Negative space affects the way shapes and objects look. What objects do you see in the picture below? Can you tell which areas are positive space and which are negative space?

 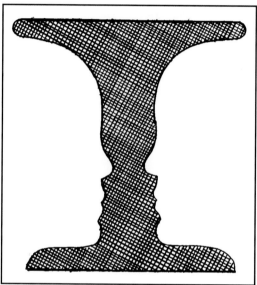

Practice

Create a design with positive and negative space. Use crayons.

1. Fold a piece of paper into two equal parts. Draw a large free-form shape on the outside of each side.

2. Use crayons to color the negative spaces only.

3. Open the paper. How do the negative spaces help you see the shapes that you drew?

Decide Did you color all the space around and between the two shapes?

Elizabeth Boger. Age 8. Tagboard, tempera, sponge.

How did this student artist create positive and negative space in her print?

Create

What shapes found in nature do you find interesting? Make a stencil print using positive and negative space.

1. Think about shapes found in nature. Draw one in the middle of stiff paper and cut it out. Keep the paper around it in one piece. This paper will be your stencil.

2. Hold the stencil in place on a large piece of paper. Dip a small piece of sponge into tempera paint and gently press it inside the stencil to make a print.

3. When the print is dry, hold the positive shape in place on the large paper. Dip the sponge into a different color. Then, gently press it around the outside edges of the positive shape.

Describe Point to the positive and negative spaces in the final design.

Analyze Which shape or stencil did you use to create the positive spaces and negative spaces?

Interpret How would your design be different if you had used only the stencil to make it?

Decide If you make another nature print someday, what will you do differently?

Depth

Artists create depth in an artwork by making objects appear close or far away.

Hughie Lee-Smith. (American). *The Piper.* 1953. Oil on composition board. 55.9 × 89.5 cm. Photograph © 1996 Detroit Institute of Arts, Gift of Mr. and Mrs. Stanley J. Winkelman. Licensed by VAGA, New York, New York.

Look at the artworks on these pages. Both artists show deep space by making the objects in the foreground large, and objects in the background smaller.

Artist unknown. (United States). *Washington's Headquarters 1780.* c. 1876. Mixed-media. $21\frac{1}{4} \times 28$ inches. National Museum of American Art. Smithsonian Institution, Washington, DC. Art Resource, New York, New York.

Study both paintings to see how the artists create depth by making objects seem near or far away.

☑ Find the objects that seem to be the closest.

☑ Which objects seem to be the furthest away?

☑ Which objects can you see most clearly?

☑ Draw a line with your finger between the front and the back of the scene. Do the objects in the front and the back look the same size?

SEEING LIKE AN ARTIST

Who looks smaller–people close to you or people farther away?

Creating Depth

Depth in an artwork is created when some objects seem to be very close and others seem to be far away.

Just like in real life, objects in artwork that are larger seem to be closer. Objects that are smaller seem to be farther away.

Just like in real life, objects in artwork that have clear, sharp edges and many details seem close. Objects that have fuzzy edges and little detail seem farther away.

Background

Foreground

Practice

Draw objects in a foreground and a background. Use colored pencils.

Decide Which object looks farther away?

1. Near the bottom of your paper, draw an animal or an object. Make it large.

2. Draw the same animal or object near the top of your paper. Make it much smaller.

Unit **3**

Ashley Davis. Age 7. *Playing Wolves.* Pencil and crayon.

How did this student artist show depth in her drawing?

Create

What are some different places where you might find animals? Create depth in a real or imaginary scene.

1. Think about a place where there are lots of animals.

2. Make a rough sketch of the animals and other objects you want in your scene. Show depth by drawing animals and objects larger in the foreground and smaller in the background.

3. Fill your scene with color.

Describe Name the animals and objects you put in the foreground. What did you put in the background?

Analyze Which objects are the largest? Which are the smallest? Why are they different sizes?

Interpret What title would you give your painting?

Decide What did you like best about this drawing? Can you say why?

Overlapping

**Artists overlap objects to make some objects
seem close and others far away.**

Joseph Jean-Gilles. (Haitian). *Haitian Landscape.* 1973. Oil on canvas. 76 × 122 cm. Collection
of the Art Museum of the Americas, Organization of American States, Washington, DC.

Look at the landscape paintings on these pages.
Joseph Jean-Gilles has overlapped houses,
trees, and gardens. He has created a picture of a
farming community. Sylvia Plimack Mangold has
added a sense of depth by painting branches that
cover each other. This makes the trees in front look
closer to the viewer.

Sylvia Plimack Mangold. (American). *The Locust Trees with Maple.* 1990. Oil on linen. Courtesy, Brooke Alexander Gallery, New York, New York.

Study both paintings to see how overlapping creates a feeling of depth.

☑ Find objects in each painting that overlap.

☑ Which branches in *The Locust Trees with Maple* look closer to you? Which look farther away?

☑ What objects cover parts of the houses in *Haitian Landscape*? What objects do the houses cover?

☑ Describe the objects in *Haitian Landscape* that look closest to you. Which look farthest away?

SEEING LIKE AN ARTIST

Look out a window and find examples of objects that overlap.

Creating Overlapping

Overlapping occurs when one object covers a part of a second object. Overlapping makes the object in front seem to be closer to the viewer.

When objects overlap, they create **depth**, or the appearance of distance, on a flat surface. The one in front appears to be closer to the viewer. The second object seems to be farther away.

Practice

Draw shapes that overlap. Use pencil or crayon.

1. Create a feeling of depth in a design by overlapping geometric shapes.

2. Draw one large shape. Then, draw a second shape so that part of it is hidden behind the large shape.

3. Add other shapes.

Decide Do some shapes look like they are in front? Do others look like they are behind?

Nick Rogers. Age 8. *The Forest.* Pencil.

How did this student artist create a feeling of depth?

Create

How do the trees look when you are walking toward them? Create a drawing of overlapping trees and branches.

1. Think about the different parts of a tree. How do the branches look? Sketch some, using different kinds of lines.

2. Draw some trees, making each tree's branches and leaves overlap to create a feeling of depth.

3. Fill your page, and touch all edges of the paper with your lines and shapes.

Describe Where did you use overlapping in your drawing?

Analyze How did overlapping help you create a feeling of depth?

Interpret How would your drawing change if the trees did not overlap?

Decide How is your drawing like the paintings shown in this lesson? How is it different?

Form

Artists use three-dimensional forms to create sculptures.

Fernand Leger. (French).
The Walking Flower. 1951.
Ceramic. $26\frac{1}{2} \times 20\frac{1}{2} \times 15$ inches.
Albright-Knox, Buffalo,
New York.

Look at the sculptures on these pages.
The Walking Flower is a clay sculpture. *The Spinner* is a metal mobile. Form is an important element in both these sculptures.

Alexander Calder. (American). *The Spinner.* 1966. Aluminum, steel, and oil paint. 235 × 351 inches. Collection Walker Art Center, Minneapolis, Gift of Dayton Hudson Corporation, Minneapolis, Minnesota.

Study both sculptures to find the following forms.

☑ Find a form that has a shape like a circle.

☑ Locate forms that look like triangles.

☑ Find free-forms in these sculptures.

SEEING LIKE AN ARTIST

Look around your classroom. Find objects that have forms like the ones you found in the artwork.

Using Form

Shapes and forms are similar. They both can be geometric or free-form. But they are different, too. **Shapes** are flat and are **two-dimensional** (2-D). They can be measured in only two ways: height and width.

Forms are not flat. They are **three-dimensional** (3-D) and can be measured in three ways: height, width, and depth.

Below are five basic forms. You saw them in the sculptures in this lesson. Which shapes do these forms remind you of?

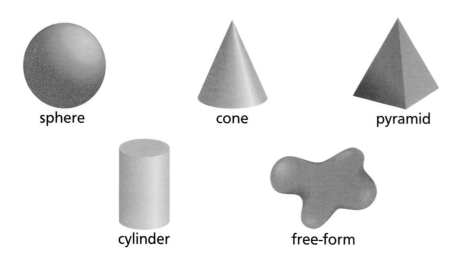

sphere   cone   pyramid

cylinder   free-form

Sculpture is art that is three-dimensional. The form of the sculpture is the positive space. The negative space is the area all around the form.

Practice

Make a form. It will have three dimensions. Use paper.

1. Tear a piece of paper in several places without tearing it completely apart.

2. Fold, bend, curl, and twist the paper to make a form. Notice that it has three-dimensions: height, width, and depth.

Decide Does your paper form have spaces inside and all around it?

Pernandas Freeman. Age 8. *Musical Free Shape.*
Construction paper and oil pastels.

How do you know this paper sculpture is 3-D?

Create

What objects around you have three dimensions? Create a three-dimensional paper sculpture.

1. Think about different ways of shaping paper.

2. Cut out a large free-form shape from a piece of construction paper. Decorate it with a variety of lines and shapes.

3. Turn your 2-D shape into a 3-D sculpture. Make several deep cuts along the outside edges toward the inside.

4. Join opposite points of the cut pieces together. Glue the points together.

Describe Point to the three dimensions in your sculpture. Identify the positive and negative spaces.

Analyze How did you change the paper to create a 3-D form?

Interpret What does your sculpture make you think of? Why are the negative spaces important to it?

Decide Which do you like better—your 2-D design or your finished sculpture?

Lesson 4

Relief Sculpture

Artists create relief sculptures by making raised forms on flat surfaces. Reliefs often are used for decoration.

Lorenzo Ghiberti. (Italian). *The Meeting of Solomon and Sheba/The Gates of Paradise.* 1425–52. Gilded bronze. Scala/Art Resource, NY.

Look at the artwork on these two pages. The bronze panel has figures that seem to be almost freestanding. This type of relief is called high relief. The *Winged Genie,* carved in Assyria around 850 B.C., is an example of low relief. Its design is slightly raised above the background.

Artist unknown. (Assyria). *Winged Genie.* c. 883–859 B.C. Alabaster. 91 inches high. Brooklyn Museum of Art, New York, New York.

Study both artworks to find the following areas of relief.

☑ Find the areas that appear to be raised. Trace them with your finger.

☑ Where are the flat background areas?

☑ Which relief seems to be the highest?

☑ Which work has a background that seems to go backward in space?

☑ In which work do the figures seems most lifelike?

SEEING LIKE AN ARTIST
Look closely at both sides of a coin. Which areas are raised? Why do you think the background is empty?

Creating Relief Sculpture

Artwork in which forms stand out from a flat surface is called **relief sculpture**.

Most three-dimensional sculptures are **freestanding**. They have empty, negative space all around them. Relief sculptures, however, are not freestanding. The background is flat. The positive areas are raised up from the background.

Coins are one example of relief that we see every day. What other examples can you think of?

Practice

Write your name in relief. Use glue and yarn.

1. Make a design with thick lines of yarn glued onto a piece of paper.

2. Allow the glue to dry for a few hours.

Decide Feel the letters of your name. Do they stand out from the surface of your paper?

Brittny Thomas. Age 9. *This is Me*. Clay.

How is this student artist's relief sculpture different from one that is freestanding?

Create

What would you like to show in a self-portrait? Create a self-portrait in relief tile.

1. Think about making a self-portrait of your face or your whole body. Draw a self-portrait on paper for practice.

2. Roll out a slab of clay. Draw your portrait into it with a pencil. Design a frame and press it into the clay around your portrait. Carve away from the area around the portrait but not the frame. Be careful not to carve all the way through the slab.

3. Use scrap pieces of clay to add details.

Describe What shapes did you use? Describe the textures.

Analyze Which areas are in relief? Where are the negative spaces?

Interpret What words would you use to describe your self-portrait? How would the work change if there were no raised areas?

Decide What do you like best? Why?

3-D Art to Wear

A jeweler creates decorative three-dimensional forms to wear.

Artist unknown. (Morocco). *Necklace.* Twentieth century. Beads and silver alloy. 14 inches long.

Compare the necklace from Morocco to the tuxedo studs and cuff links. They are all forms of three-dimensional art, or jewelry. These pieces of jewelry also have raised areas and a variety of materials.

Iris Sandkühler. *Tuxedo Studs and Cufflinks.* 1994. The Joseph Robbins Collection.

Study both works of art.

- ✓ Find areas where the designs are raised.
- ✓ Find the jewelry that has beads made from coral.
- ✓ How will the necklace sound when worn?
- ✓ Which piece has a variety of raised jewels?

SEEING LIKE AN ARTIST
Look around your classroom. Is anyone wearing jewelry? What color is it? What materials is it made of?

Designing and Making Jewelry

A piece of **jewelry** is three-dimensional artwork that is made for people to wear. A **jeweler** is an artist who designs and makes jewelry. The art of making jewelry has been around for about 4000 years. Rings and necklaces are forms of jewelry. Can you think of any other forms?

A variety of materials can be used to make jewelry. Gold, silver, and gemstones are used most often. Jewelry can also be made with wood, glass, leather, beads, and paper. Can you think of any other materials that can be used to make jewelry?

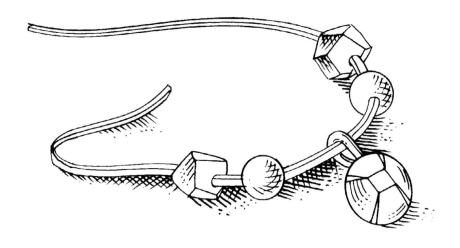

Practice

Use a found object and foil to practice making a foil relief.

1. Place foil on top of an object such as a button to get the feel of stretching foil gently. Start in the middle and use your fingertips to gently press and smooth the foil across the flat surface and over the ridges.

2. Remove the foil from the object and you will have the object's impression.

Decide Does the impression of the object show in the foil?

Megan Stein. Age 8. *Raised Rounds.* Posterboard, aluminum foil, ink.

What makes this medallion a relief?

Create

What type of jewelry would you like to wear? Create a medallion.

1. Think about small objects that have interesting shapes.

2. Cut cardboard into a geometric shape. Arrange objects in different ways on top. Glue down your favorite arrangement.

3. When dry, cover the surface with foil.

4. Punch a hole at the top of your design. Pass a piece of yarn or ribbon through the hole and tie the ends.

Describe What objects did you use to create the areas of the relief?

Analyze Why are some areas lower than other areas?

Interpret When would you wear your medallion?

Decide If you could create another medallion, what would you change?

Lesson 6

Space and Form in Dance

American Indian Dance Theatre:
"Hoop Dance."

an artist creates shapes and forms with paint on paper. A dancer creates shapes and forms through movement. This dancer is dancing the Native American "Hoop Dance." The dancer uses reed hoops to create forms in the air. He creates the form of a butterfly, a turtle, flowers, a snake, and a globe.

What To Do

Create movements to show the ideas in a poem.

Materials

None

1. Read the Navajo poem aloud. Its theme is a love of nature.

2. Talk about what you think the poem means.

3. Work with a partner. Design a movement to show each line in the poem. You are creating forms and shapes with the movements of your body.

4. When you are ready, perform the poem while your partner says the lines. Then, say the lines while your partner performs the poem.

In beauty, I walk
With beauty before me.
I walk with beauty
   behind me.
I walk with beauty
   beside me.
I walk with beauty
   above me.
I walk with beauty
   below me.
With beauty all around
   me, I walk.
With beauty within me,
   I walk.
It is finished in beauty.

Describe What gestures did you make to show the idea of each line?

Analyze Explain how your movements create forms and shapes.

Interpret Identify the feelings that you created through your poem.

Decide How well did you succeed in matching your movements to the words of the poem?

Extra Credit · · · · · · · · · · · · · · · ·

Design a costume to be worn as you perform the poem. Use things that you can find at home or school.

Space and Form

Reviewing Main Ideas

The lessons and activities in this unit cover the techniques that artists use to create space and form.

1. **Positive space** is the area that shapes and forms fill.

2. **Negative space** is the empty area between and around the shapes or objects.

3. **Depth** in an artwork is created when some objects seem to be very close and others seem to be far away.

   - **Foreground** is the part of the picture that appears closest to the viewer.

   - **Background** is the part that appears farthest away.

Henry Moore. (British). *Knife Edge Mirror Two Piece.* 1977–1978. Bronze. $210\frac{1}{2} \times 284 \times 143$ inches. © 1996 Board of Trustees, National Gallery of Art, Washington, DC. Gift of the Morris and Gwendolyn Cafritz Foundation.

4. **Overlapping** is when one object covers a part of a second object.

5. **Shapes** are flat and two-dimensional. They can be measured by height and width.

6. **Forms** are shapes that are three-dimensional. They can be measured by height, width, and depth. (spheres, cones, pyramids, cylinders, and free-forms)

7. **Relief sculpture** is artwork in which forms stand out from a flat surface.

8. **Freestanding sculpture** is three-dimensional and has negative space all around it.

   • **Jewelry** is three-dimensional art that people wear as decoration. A *jeweler* is the artist who designs and makes it.

Summing Up

Look at the sculpture by Moore. Notice how he uses some of the techniques you learned about in this unit.

- How do you know this work of art is three-dimensional?

- Is it relief sculpture or freestanding sculpture? Explain your answer.

- What shapes and forms do the positive and negative spaces remind you of?

Space and form are important elements in works of art. By using techniques to create space and form, artists express to others what they see.

Careers in Art
City Planner

Andrew Aidt is a city planner for Kettering, Ohio. City planners plan the development of new cities or changes in existing cities. They must determine what the future population will be. They also consider what people will need in terms of housing, schools, parking space, and parks, and where these facilities should be. The main purpose of his work is to create environments that are both pleasant and practical.

Andrew Aidt, city planner

Unit 4

An Introduction to

Balance and Emphasis

Artists use balance and emphasis to design works of art.

Artist unknown. (Greek). *Parthenon.* 447–438 B.C. Marble. 237 × 110 × 60 feet. The Acropolis, Athens, Greece. Scala, Art Resource.

Artists use **balance** in their artwork to give equal weight to both sides of a design.

- How are the left and the right sides of the Parthenon the same?

- Are both sides *exactly* the same? If not, what are some differences?

Artists use **emphasis** in their artwork to create a center of interest.

- Which area of the building attracts your attention first?

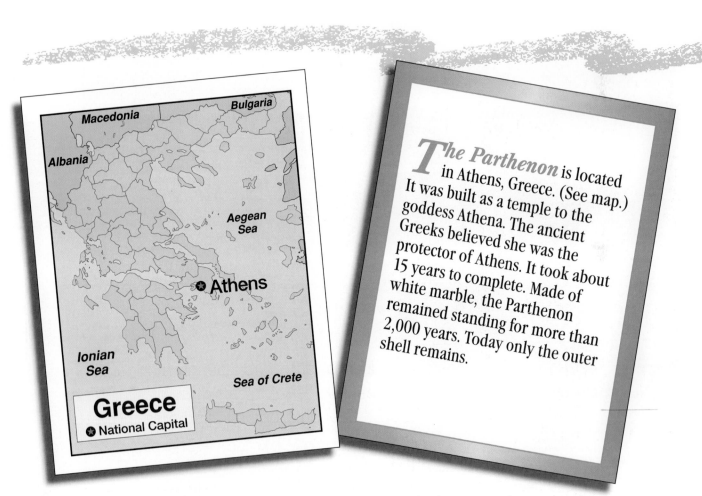

The Parthenon is located in Athens, Greece. (See map.) It was built as a temple to the goddess Athena. The ancient Greeks believed she was the protector of Athens. It took about 15 years to complete. Made of white marble, the Parthenon remained standing for more than 2,000 years. Today only the outer shell remains.

The Parthenon architects and other artists use balance and emphasis in their designs. In this unit you will learn about techniques that artists use to create balance and emphasis. The topics are:

- Formal Balance • Symmetry • Approximate Symmetry • Emphasis

Formal Balance

Sometimes artists use formal balance
in the design of their art.

Horace Pippin. (American). *Victorian Parlor II.* 1945. Oil on canvas. $25\frac{1}{4} \times 30$ inches.
The Metropolitan Museum of Art, New York, New York, Arthur Hoppock Heam Fund, 1958.

Compare the artwork on these pages.
Victorian Parlor II was painted by folk artist
Horace Pippin. Folk artists learn from the people and
works of art around them rather than by studying at
school. The *Jar* was created almost 900 years before
Victorian Parlor II, yet both works make powerful use
of formal balance.

Artist unknown. China. *Jar.* Northern Song Period, twelfth century. Stoneware with sgraffito design in slip under glaze. 12$\frac{1}{2}$ inches. The Asian Society, New York. Mr. and Mrs. John D. Rockefeller 3rd Collection/Photo by Lynton Gardiner.

Study each artwork to find the following examples of formal balance.

✓ Draw a line down the middle of each artwork with your finger. Describe the matching objects or shapes you see on either side of the line.

✓ Describe colors that are repeated in the same way in Pippin's artwork.

✓ What areas are *exactly* the same on both sides of each piece?

✓ Which areas are similar but *not* exactly the same?

SEEING LIKE AN ARTIST

Look for a building in your neighborhood that has the same colors and forms on its left and right halves. What is similar but not exactly the same?

Using Formal Balance

Formal balance is a way of organizing a design so that equal or very similar elements are placed on opposite sides of an imaginary, central dividing line. You saw examples of formal balance in the artwork on pages 106 and 107.

On a seesaw, if your partner is much bigger than you, you will stay up in the air. The seesaw is *not* balanced. But if your partner is about your weight, the seesaw will be balanced. There is about the same amount of weight on both sides.

There are different kinds of balance in a work of art. One kind is formal balance. This is created when objects, shapes, lines, and color match on both sides of a design.

Practice

Illustrate formal balance. Use pencil.

1. Fold a piece of paper in half and then open it up again. Use pencil to draw some geometric and free-form shapes on the left-hand side.

2. Repeat the same design on the right side to create formal balance.

Decide Does your design look the same on both sides?

Keegan Faught. Age 9. *House for Horace Pippin's People*. Marker and oil pastel.

Where did this student artist use formal balance?
Where did he add objects that do not use formal balance?

Create

How do buildings show formal balance? Use formal balance in a drawing.

1. Look at the artwork *Victorian Parlor II* by Horace Pippin. Think about how the outside of this house might look.

2. On a large piece of paper, draw the outside of the house. Use formal balance in your picture.

3. Fill the house with color. Add trees and plants. Use formal balance in your landscape, also.

Describe What shapes did you use? Describe the lines. Name the colors.

Analyze How did you create formal balance in your drawing?

Interpret How would the mood or feeling of your drawing change if you had not used formal balance?

Decide If you could redo this drawing, what would you do differently?

Formal Balance in Masks

Artists from different cultures use formal balance in the design of masks.

Artist unknown. Abelam (Papua New Guinea). *Yam Mask.* Nineteenth century. Yam fibers. $18\frac{3}{4} \times 13\frac{3}{8}$ inches. Nelson-Atkins Museum of Art, Kansas City, Missouri. Gift of the May Dept. Stores Co.

Look at the three-dimensional masks on these pages. The *Yam Mask* was woven from basketry materials. The *Dancing Headdress Frontlet* is carved in wood from a maple tree. Beautiful abalone shells are pressed into the wood for decoration. Both artists have used formal balance to design their masks.

Albert Edward Edensaw.
Kaigani Haida. *Dancing Headdress Frontlet.* 1860–1870.
Maple and abalone shell.
$6\frac{1}{4} \times 5\frac{7}{8} \times 2\frac{1}{4}$ inches.
The Seattle Art Museum, Seattle, Washington. Gift of John H. Hauberg. Photo by Paul Macapia.

Study both masks to find examples of formal balance.

☑ What shapes do you see in the middle of each mask?

☑ Find shapes or objects on the left side that you also see on the right.

☑ Find areas that are *exactly* the same on both sides.

☑ Which areas are *not* exactly the same on both sides?

☑ How would you describe the expression on each mask?

SEEING LIKE AN ARTIST
Look at posters and signs in your school to find examples of formal balance.

Using Formal Balance in Masks

People from around the world have many different **cultures**, or customs. Many have been making and wearing masks for thousands of years. **Masks** are sculptured faces. We believe ancient hunters wore animal masks in good-luck ceremonies before the hunt. Storytellers and actors wore masks to play different characters. Warriors used them for protection. Masks are still being made and worn today.

Masks' features often are **exaggerated**, or made bigger, to show strong feelings. Which features are exaggerated on the masks below? What feelings do they seem to express?

The masks below have **formal balance**. They have the same elements on both sides of a central, imaginary dividing line.

Practice

Design a simple paper mask with exaggerated features formally balanced. Use colored markers.

1. Fold a piece of paper in half and then open it up again to mark the middle of the mask.

2. Think of a feeling you want the mask to express. Sketch exaggerated features that express it, using free-form and geometric shapes. The features on each side of the fold should look alike in some way.

Analyze Which features did you exaggerate? Why did you choose to exaggerate them? Which are formally balanced?

Max Manofsky. Age 8. *M. M. M. Dracula.*
Papier-mâché and tempera.

What part of this student artist's
mask shows exaggeration?

Create

What features in a mask would show formal balance? Create a papier-mâché mask using formal balance.

1. Think of how you want to use your mask and what it will express. Make a few sketches until you get one you like.

2. Look at your sketch. Then, cut pieces of cardboard tubes and boxes to form the features. Tape or glue them in place onto your base, formally balancing some forms.

3. Apply torn strips of newspaper dipped in paste to the mask.

4. When your mask is dry, paint it. Balance colors and lines.

Describe Name the forms and colors that you used.

Analyze What gives the mask formal balance? Which features are most exaggerated? Why did you choose to exaggerate them?

Interpret What feeling does the finished mask express?

Decide Which elements of the mask do you like best? How is the finished mask different from your sketch?

Symmetry

Symmetry is a special type of formal balance in which both sides of a piece of artwork are exactly the same.

Artist unknown. *Symmetrical View of a Totem Pole.* Photo. © Ron Watts/Westlight. Stanley Park. Vancouver-B.C., Canada.

A totem is the sacred symbol of an animal whose spirit represents and protects a family clan. They were placed in front of homes. The totems on both these pages were carved into tall, wooden poles by artists. Animals most often used in totems include the thunderbird, raven, eagle, bear, frog, wolf, and beaver.

Artist unknown. *Symmetrical View of a Totem Pole.*
Photo. © Matthew McVay/Tony Stone Images, Inc.
Stanley Park. Vancouver-B.C., Canada.

Study both sculptures to find examples of symmetry.

✓ What single shape or object do you see in the center of each carving?

✓ Find the shapes that are exactly the same on both sides of the center line.

✓ What colors are repeated in exactly the same place on both sides of the center?

SEEING LIKE AN ARTIST

Look at the artwork in this book to find other examples of symmetry.

Using Symmetry

These artists used symmetry to design the faces and bodies of the animals on the totems. **Symmetry** is a special type of formal balance in which two halves of a design are identical, mirror images of each other. The two halves are divided by a **central axis**, which is an imaginary dividing line. Everything on one side of the central axis is balanced by the other side.

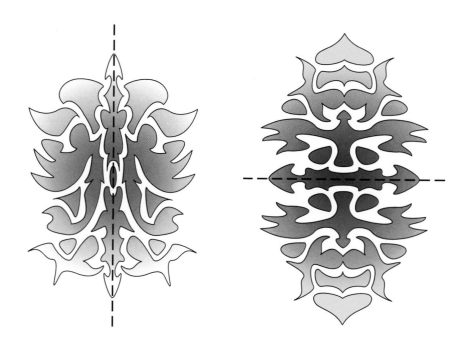

The formal balance of the designs on the totems gives a feeling of calm and dignity. The tall vertical form adds a feeling of importance. Artists use symmetry when they want designs to look formal and important.

Practice

Use a balance scale to create perfect balance. Use a variety of materials.

Practice formal balance by adding and taking away a variety of materials on each side of the scale.

Decide Can you create perfect balance?

Find the central axis in this student artist's totem.

Donald Nguyen. Age 9. *Creatures of the Night.* Cut paper.

Create

What images would you put on a totem pole? Use symmetry to create a totem.

1. Think of a real or imaginary creature. Make several sketches.

2. Fold a sheet of paper in half. The fold will be your central axis.

3. Using small pieces of colored paper, cut out shapes to represent features such as eyes. Place these features on your totem using symmetry. Glue the pieces into place.

4. Use symmetry to add other details.

5. Join the edges of your paper together to form a cylinder.

Describe What creature did you choose for your totem? What kinds of shapes are used?

Analyze How did you create symmetrical balance?

Interpret What kind of feeling does the formal balance give your totem?

Decide If you could create another totem, what would you do differently?

Approximate Symmetry

Artists can use symmetry to balance their designs.

Artist unknown. (Egypt). *Portrait of a Boy.* Second century A.D. 38 × 19 cm. Encaustic on wood. The Metropolitan Museum of Art, New York. Gift of Edward S. Harkness, 1918.

Look at the portraits on these pages. *Portrait of a Boy* is a painting from an Egyptian mummy case created more than 1,800 years ago. *Her World* was painted in 1948. Both artists have used approximate symmetry to create these portraits. When something is symmetrical, it is the same on both sides. Approximate symmetry means that something is almost the same on both sides.

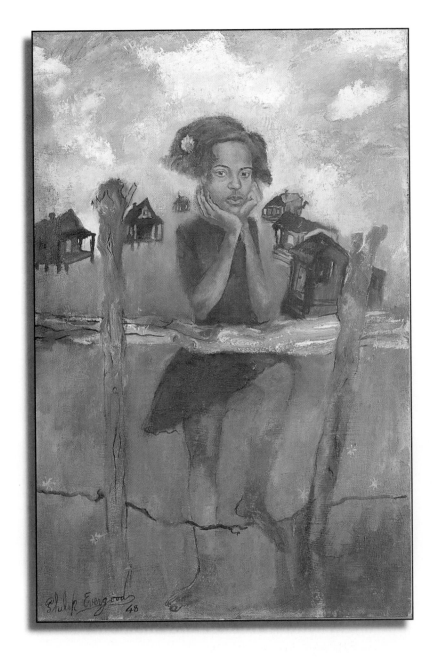

Philip Evergood. (American).
Her World. 1948. Oil on canvas.
$48 \times 35\frac{5}{8}$ inches. The Metropolitan
Museum of Art, New York.

Study each painting to find the following examples
of approximate symmetry.

✓ Which features on the left side of the face are
exactly the same as the ones on the right?

✓ Locate the shapes that are almost the same on
both sides of the face.

✓ In which portrait is the hair the same on both sides
of the middle?

Look at a friend's
face to find examples
of approximate
symmetry.

Using Approximate Symmetry

Approximate symmetry is a special kind of formal balance that happens when both sides of a design are *almost* exactly the same. The human face has approximate symmetry. Both sides are almost exactly the same.

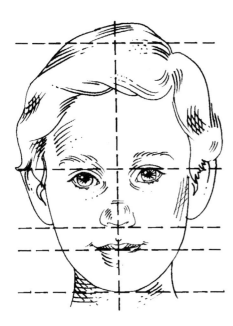

When drawing a portrait, it is helpful to draw the shape of the head first. Look at the **guidelines** in the face above. You can see that the eyes are placed about halfway between the top of the head and the bottom of the chin. Where do you find the tops of the ears? The nose? The mouth? What about your own face?

Practice

Illustrate approximate symmetry. Use pencil.

1. Create the shape of a head by drawing a large oval shape. Draw a line *down* the middle and also *across* the middle of the shape.

2. Look at the guidelines in the diagram above to help you place the eyes, nose, mouth, and ears.

Decide Does the face show approximate symmetry?

How did this student artist create approximate symmetry?

Daria Crenshaw. Age 8. *Self-Portrait of Daria*. Tempera.

Create

What parts of your face show approximate symmetry? Use approximate symmetry in a self-portrait.

1. Look at your face in the mirror. Notice how it is almost exactly the same on both sides.

2. Draw a self-portrait using approximate symmetry.

3. In the spaces around your portrait, draw objects that are important to you.

4. Add color.

Describe What shapes did you use to create the face? What objects are included in the background?

Analyze How did you create approximate symmetry in the face?

Interpret How would the face look if you had not used approximate symmetry?

Decide If you had painted this self-portrait a year ago, what objects would you have included?

Lesson 4

Emphasis

Artists use emphasis in their artwork to create a center of interest.

Yvonne Jacquette. (American).
Tokyo Street with Pachinko Parlor II.
1985. Oil on canvas. $85\frac{5}{16} \times 55\frac{3}{16}$ inches.
Courtesy, Yvonne Jacquette and
the D C Moore Gallery.

Look at the artworks on these pages. Yvonne Jacquette painted *Tokyo Street with Pachinko Parlor II* in 1985. French artist Edgar Degas created his artwork about 100 years earlier. Both artists used emphasis to create a center of interest in their work. They did this by showing a contrast of light and dark values.

Edgar Degas. (France). *Waiting.* c. 1882. 19 × 24 inches. Pastel on paper. Jointly owned by the Norton Simon Museum, Pasadena, California, and The J. Paul Getty Museum Malibu, Pasadena, CA.

Study both artworks to find areas of emphasis.

Find which areas attract your attention most.

Where do you see the lightest areas?

Find the darkest areas.

Do the two artworks give you different feelings? Describe the differences.

Understanding Emphasis

Sometimes an artist wants you to look immediately at a certain area in a work of art. This area is called the **center of interest**. An artist uses **emphasis** to draw your attention there. Often, the center of interest shows the artist's main idea.

Contrast is one way to emphasize a center of interest. This can be used when there is a great difference between two things, such as a contrast in **value**. This is shown in the following examples. The area with strong value contrasts, lightness or darkness of a color, will attract your attention first.

Practice

Contrast values to illustrate emphasis. Use pencil and black crayon.

1. Draw a shape several times until a small piece of paper is filled. Keep the shapes about the same size.

2. Pick one to be the center of interest. Color it with black crayon, leaving the rest of the shapes uncolored to create emphasis.

Analyze Which shape attracts your attention first? Why?

Mara Santiago. Age 8. Dustless chalk.

What did this student artist use as the center of interest in her night scene?

Create

What would you emphasize in a night scene? Contrast value to show the center of interest in a drawing.

1. On black paper, use a piece of colored chalk to draw a picture of your house or apartment at night. Choose one object or a small group of objects you want to emphasize.

2. To make your chosen object the center of interest, color it with light colors.

3. Use dark values for contrast to color the rest of the objects in your picture.

Describe What objects did you include in your drawing? Where are the light areas? Where are the dark areas?

Analyze How did you use emphasis to create a center of interest?

Interpret How would the mood or feeling of your artwork change if you had used light values only?

Decide What else could you draw and show a center of interest?

Emphasis Through Contrast in Shapes

Artists can contrast shapes to create a center of interest in a work of art.

Allan Houser. (American). *Apache Crown Dance.* 1953. Casein. 24 $\frac{5}{8}$ × 36 $\frac{1}{2}$ inches. The Denver Art Museum, Denver, Colorado.

Look at the paintings on these pages. Allan Houser painted *Apache Crown Dance* in 1953. About 40 years later, Jane Freilicher painted *The Sun Breaks Through*. The subject matter in each is very different, but both artists used emphasis to create a center of interest. They did this by showing a contrast in the size of the shapes.

Jane Freilicher. (American). *The Sun Breaks Through.* 1991. Oil on linen.
$47 \times 49\frac{1}{2}$ inches. Private Collection. Courtesy, Fischbach Gallery, New York.

Study both paintings to find areas of emphasis.

- Where do you see the active shapes?

- Which areas or objects attract your attention most?

- Find the artwork that has small shapes in the center of interest.

- Which painting uses large shapes in the center of interest? Where are the smaller shapes in this work?

SEEING LIKE AN ARTIST

Look around on the ground outside. Find an object completely surrounded by shapes that are the opposite size.

Emphasis Through Contrasts

Using **emphasis** through contrast in shape is one way to create a center of interest in a work of art.

Artists can emphasize a center of interest by **contrasting** values. They can also create emphasis by contrasting shapes and sizes. A large shape, for example, will stand out if it is surrounded by small shapes.

A free-form shape will attract attention first if it is surrounded by geometric shapes.

Practice

Illustrate contrast in shape. Use crayon.

1. Fold a piece of paper into two equal parts. On the left side, draw a free-form shape. Draw geometric shapes around it.

2. On the right side, draw a large circle. Draw smaller circles around it.

Decide Which shapes first attract your attention? Why?

Carla Sutton. Age 8. *Falling Leaves*. Construction paper.

Which leaf is emphasized in this student artist's collage?

Create

What would you emphasize in a collage of leaves? Contrast shapes to show emphasis in a collage.

1. Think of leaves from trees, houseplants, or other plants you remember. Sketch some that have different shapes.

2. Draw leaves on different colors of paper. Draw one leaf very large and the others much smaller. Cut them out.

3. The large leaf will be your center of interest. Arrange all the leaves on a piece of black construction paper. Fill the page. Glue the leaves down. Add details with oil pastels.

Describe What shapes did you use in your collage? Name the colors. Describe the lines. Where is the center of interest?

Analyze How did you emphasize the center of interest?

Interpret How would the feeling of your collage change if all the shapes were the same size?

Decide Which shapes do you like best? Why? Which ones would you change? Why?

Balance and Emphasis in Pantomime

The Chameleons: Sharon Diskin and Keith Berger.

a mime tells a story without words. Mimes communicate with the movements of their bodies and the expressions on their faces. Sometimes a mime copies another person. The two people are balanced, as one does just what the other does. The mime is like your image in a mirror.

What To Do

Mirror some of your daily activities with a partner.

Materials

None

1. Work with a partner. Face each other and practice moving as though you are the mirror image of your partner. Take turns.

2. Choose four simple, everyday activities to mime. Each partner can lead two activities. You might comb your hair, put on clothes, draw a picture, or make a sandwich. Move very slowly, using clear gestures and movement.

3. Perform your mirror study for others. Work as a team. You and your partner should do exactly the same things.

Describe How did you use mime to show everyday activities?

Analyze Explain how you made certain that you and your partner balanced each other.

Interpret Tell how your actions expressed the mood or feeling of an everyday activity.

Decide Were you satisfied with your activities? Were you more successful as a leader or as a follower? Why?

Extra Credit

Choose an everyday activity to mime. Design it so that it has a beginning, a middle, and an end. Perform it for others.

Balance and Emphasis

Reviewing Main Ideas

The lessons and activities in this unit cover the techniques that artists use to create balance and emphasis.

1. **Formal balance** is a way of organizing a design so that equal or very similar elements are placed on opposite sides of a central dividing line. Many *masks* are examples of formal balance.

2. **Symmetry** is a type of formal balance in which both sides of a design are *exactly* the same. The two halves are divided by a *central axis,* an imaginary dividing line.

3. **Approximate symmetry** is a special kind of formal balance in which both sides of a design are *almost* exactly the same.

4. **Emphasis** is the way artists create a **center of interest** in their artwork. Following are two common ways to create emphasis.

- **Contrast in value** — A light area will attract attention if there are darker areas around it.

- **Contrast in shape** — Large shapes will stand out if they are surrounded by smaller shapes.

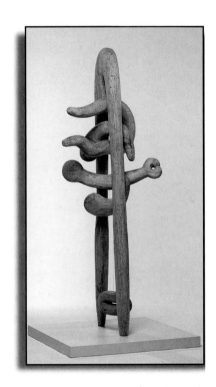

Isamu Noguchi. (American). *Cronos.* 1947. Wood, string, metal. $86\frac{1}{4} \times 22 \times 31$ inches. Collection Walker Art Center, Minneapolis, Minnesota, Gift of the artist, 1979.

Summing Up

Cronos is a wooden sculpture by American artist Isamu Noguchi. In this sculpture, Noguchi used the techniques of balance and emphasis covered in this unit.

- Which type of formal balance did the artist use to design this sculpture? Give a reason for your answer.
- Find the center of interest in this sculpture.
- Which of the two techniques did Noguchi use to create emphasis?

Balance and **emphasis** are important design principles in art. By using techniques to create emphasis, artists can create a center of interest in their artwork.

Let's Visit a Museum

The Walker Art Center, located in Minneapolis, Minnesota, is famous for its collection of 8,000 pieces of twentieth-century art. The collection includes paintings, sculpture, videos, prints, drawings, and photographs. The Walker Art Center also has a varied educational program that appeals to people of all ages. Beside the museum is the Minneapolis Sculpture Garden. It covers 11 acres and is one of the largest urban sculpture parks in the country. It is a popular tourist attraction.

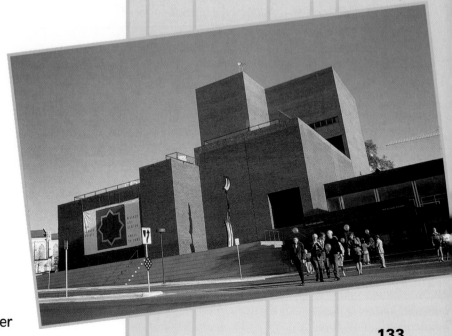

The Walker Art Center

An Introduction to
Texture and Rhythm

Artists create texture and rhythm to show
how things move and feel.

Artist unknown. *Bayeux Tapestry*. Detail of *Norman Cavalry Charging in the
Battle of Hastings*. 1070–1080. Embroidered wool on linen.
20 inches high × 231 feet. Musée de Peinture, Bayeux, France.
Art Resource, New York, New York.

Artists can create **texture** in a work of art to show how things feel, or look as if they might feel if touched.

- If you were able to touch the surface of the *Bayeux Tapestry*, how do you think it would feel?

Artists use **rhythm** in their artwork to create a feeling of movement.

- What shapes or objects do you see more than once?
- What shapes or objects look like they are moving?

Artist Profile

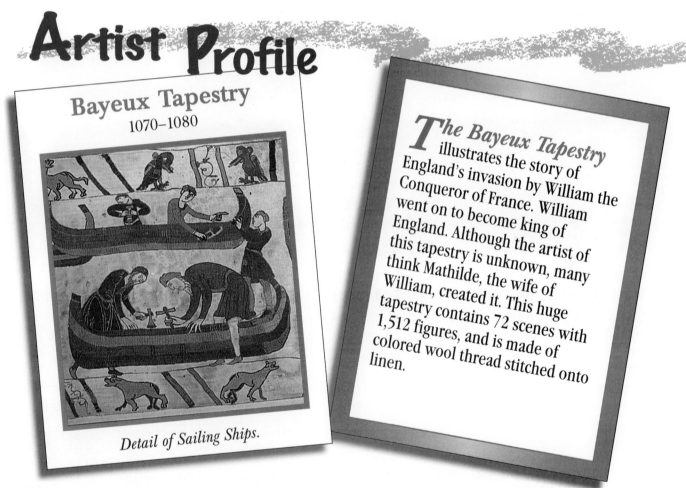

Bayeux Tapestry
1070–1080

Detail of Sailing Ships.

The *Bayeux Tapestry* illustrates the story of England's invasion by William the Conqueror of France. William went on to become king of England. Although the artist of this tapestry is unknown, many think Mathilde, the wife of William, created it. This huge tapestry contains 72 scenes with 1,512 figures, and is made of colored wool thread stitched onto linen.

The artist who created the *Bayeux Tapestry* and other artists use texture and rhythm to show how things move and feel. In this unit you will learn and practice the techniques that artists use to create texture and rhythm in their artwork. The topics are:

- Tactile Texture
- Visual Texture
- Random Rhythm
- Regular Rhythm
- Alternating Rhythm

Texture

Artists create texture in their artwork to show how objects might feel if you touched them.

Artist unknown. (Brazil). *Feather Headdress.* Early twentieth century. Reeds, palm-leaf spines, cotton cord, and macaw feathers. $23\frac{1}{4} \times 30\frac{3}{4}$ inches. Courtesy of the Smithsonian National Museum of the American Indian, NY. Collected by Frances Gow-Smith. Photo by David Heald.

Look at the artworks on these pages. The feather headdress from Brazil was made in the early 1900s. It was part of a costume worn in a special ceremony. The colorful shirt was woven in Peru about 1,000 years earlier. Texture is an important element in both works of art. What do you think they would feel like if you could touch them?

Artist unknown. Coastal Huari (Peru). *Shirt Section.* c. A.D. 600–1000. Alpaca wool and cotton. 21 × 12⅞ inches. The Metropolitan Museum of Art, The Michael C. Rockefeller Memorial Collection, bequest of Nelson A. Rockefeller, 1979, New York, New York.

Study the textures of both works of art.

☑ Look at the yellow-orange areas in both pieces. How do the different textures change the way the color looks?

☑ How do the orange areas in the headdress look different from the orange areas in the shirt?

☑ If you could touch the red in each artwork, in what way would they feel different?

SEEING LIKE AN ARTIST
Look around your classroom. Find objects that are smooth or rough.

Using Texture

Texture is the way the surface of an object feels or *looks* as if it would feel if you could touch it. You saw examples of different textures in the artwork on pages 136–137.

Every surface has a texture. You can feel the texture of an object by touching it.

Furry, bumpy, smooth, and *rough* are just a few of the words that describe texture. Look at the objects below. What words would you use to describe how each object might feel if you touched it?

| furry | bumpy | smooth | rough |

Textures can also change the way *colors* look. For example, red looks different on a carpet than it does on a shiny new bicycle.

Practice

Compare and contrast the way a color looks on different objects. Use found objects.

1. Find two objects that are about the same color but have different textures. One of the objects should have a rough or bumpy texture. The other object should be smooth.

2. What words describe the texture of each? How does texture affect the look of the color?

Decide What differences do you see in the way the colors look?

Sean Cunningham. Age 8. *The Night in the Mountains.* Felt, woven fabric, white cardboard, a feather, and burlap on black posterboard.

What materials did this student artist use to create a mixed-media collage?

Create

What textures could you use in a collage? Create a mixed-media collage.

1. Think about interesting textures. Collect as many materials as you can that have related colors but different textures.

2. Cut some of your texture samples into simple shapes—such as circles and triangles—of different sizes.

3. Arrange the shapes in different ways. Cut some of your samples, if necessary, to improve your design. Select the best arrangement, filling your entire cardboard with texture. Glue the pieces into place.

Describe Describe the textures of the materials you used.

Analyze How do the different textures change the look of the color?

Interpret Think of words to describe the mood of the collage.

Decide If you could make another multimedia texture collage, what would you do differently?

Tactile Texture

Artists may use a variety of tactile textures in their work.

Artist unknown. Absaroke (United States). *Thunderbird Shield.*
c. 1830. Buffalo hide shield with inner cover decorated with
paintings and feathers. Courtesy of the Smithsonian National
Museum of the American Indian, NY. Collected by W. Wildschut.
Photo by David Heald.

Look at the works of art on these pages. *Thunderbird Shield* was made more than 100 years before the appliqué. The artist created it to wear when hunting or fighting and in special ceremonies. *Various Fish* is a fabric **appliqué** designed and stitched by Ayako Miyawaki. Both artists used a number of tactile textures in their work.

Ayako Miyawaki. (Japanese). *Various Fish.* 1967. $13 \times 11\frac{3}{4}$ inches. Cotton collage on burlap. The National Museum of Women in the Arts, Washington, DC. Gift of the artist.

Study both artworks to find tactile textures.

✓ Locate the smooth fabrics and the smooth-looking animal skin.

✓ Find the bumpy lines and dots made with string. How would they feel if you could touch them?

✓ Which artwork was made to look at and which was made for a particular function?

SEEING LIKE AN ARTIST
Look through the artwork in this book. Find a work of art that includes real textures.

Using Tactile Texture

Tactile texture is the way the surface of an object *actually* feels when you touch it. It is an important element in many forms of art. Tactile textures are often the first things noticed in sculptures, jewelry, and weavings. Textured papers and fabrics make the surface of a drawing more interesting. Materials such as feathers and sand in a painting call attention to the rich variety of textures in our world.

Some artists use appliqué to create tactile texture. **Appliqué** is an art form in which cutout fabrics are attached to a larger surface.

Architects use tactile textures such as wood, brick, glass, and stone in designing buildings.

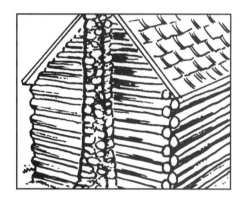
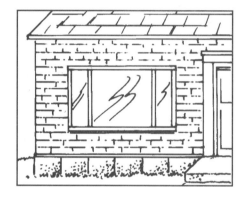

Interior designers use tactile textures in furniture, carpets, and curtains to decorate the inside of a building. What textures are on the outside of the building where you live? What textures do you have in your bedroom or kitchen?

Practice

Look carefully at tactile textures in your clothing.

1. Find different textures in your clothing.

2. Describe how each texture feels when you touch it.

Decide What words come to mind when you touch each object?

Tawny Kern. Age 8. *All About Me.* Burlap and marker.

What does this appliqué banner tell you about the student artist?

Create

What symbol would you choose to represent yourself? Design and stitch an appliqué banner.

1. Think about symbols that represent you. Make several sketches.

2. Choose your best sketch as a model. Cut out shapes from colorful fabric. Arrange them onto a piece of burlap.

3. Attach shapes using glue. Stitch around the edges of each shape and add details with marker.

Describe Name the different materials and tactile textures in your artwork. Describe how the textures feel when you touch them.

Analyze How did you organize the shapes on your banner?

Interpret How do the shapes in the banner represent you?

Decide What do you like best about your artwork?

Lesson 2

Visual Texture

Artists can create visual texture in their work.

Audrey Flack (American). *Buddha*. 1975. Airbrushed acrylic over polymer emulsion on canvas. 70 × 96 inches. Purchase: Contemporary Art Society and Tax Funds, The Saint Louis Art Museum, St. Louis, Missouri.

Study the paintings on these pages. Artist Audrey Flack's *Buddha* is a still-life painting that looks as real as a photograph. See how she makes the beads appear to shine. The portrait of King Louis XV was painted by Hyacinthe Rigaud 260 years earlier. He is best known for painting people in the royal court in France. Notice how he has created the visual texture of fur.

Hyacinthe Rigaud. (French).
Portrait of Louis XV as a Child. 1715.
Oil on canvas. 1.89 × 1.35 meters.
Giraudon/Art Resource, New York,
New York.

Look closely at both paintings to find visual textures.

✓ Find the textures that look smooth.

✓ Where are the furry-looking textures?

✓ Find the bumpy textures and shiny objects.

SEEING LIKE AN ARTIST
Find the shiniest object in your classroom. What makes it look so shiny?

Using Visual Texture

Visual texture is texture you see with your eyes.

Rub the surface of the pictures below with your fingers. You cannot actually feel the different textures. You feel the smoothness of the paper instead.

If you have felt these textures before, you probably remember how they feel. Your eyes "see" the textures even though you cannot actually feel them. This is called visual texture.

Artists show shiny surfaces by using highlights. **Highlights** are small areas of white used to show the very brightest spots on an object.

Practice

Make a rubbing of a texture to illustrate visual texture. Use pencil.

1. Find an example of texture in your classroom.

2. Place a piece of paper on top of the object. Use the side of a pencil to rub the surface of the paper to create visual texture.

Decide What lines, shapes, or values help you see the texture of the object on your paper?

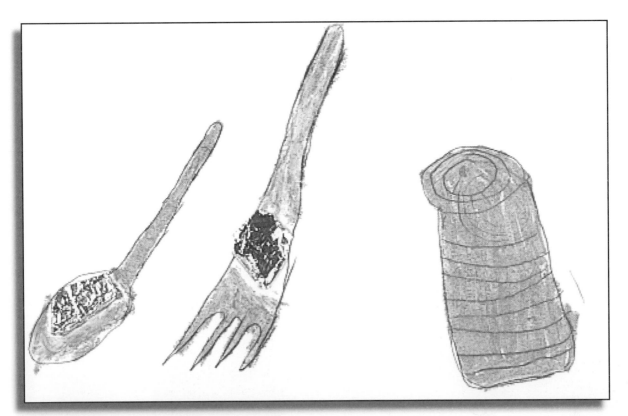

Trina Clemens. Age 8. *Shiny.* Mixed-media.

How did this student artist show visual texture?

Create

What shiny objects can you think of? Draw a still life of shiny objects showing their visual textures.

1. Think about shiny objects of different shapes and sizes. Work in small groups to collect and arrange them into a still life.

2. Draw the still life you arranged. Make the shapes large.

3. Look for the brightest parts. Glue pieces of aluminum foil onto the shapes that you drew to show where the brightest parts are.

4. Color the rest of the shapes with oil pastels.

Describe What objects did you use for your still life?

Analyze How did you use shiny visual texture in your drawing?

Interpret What is the mood or feeling of this drawing? How would the feeling change if you took out the highlights and shadows?

Decide If you could do this artwork over again, what would you do differently?

Random Rhythm

Artists use random rhythm to create a
feeling of movement in their work.

Oscar Claude Monet. (French). *Water Lilies.* 1905. Oil on canvas.
$35\frac{1}{4} \times 39\frac{1}{2}$ inches. Museum of Fine Arts, Gift of Jackson Holmes,
Boston, Massachusetts.

Compare the paintings on these pages.
Claude Monet painted water lilies growing
in his garden. Martha Walter painted a scene
showing people from other countries who had
just arrived in the United States around 1922.
Both artists used random rhythms in the design
of their work.

Martha Walter. (American). *The Telegram, Detention Room, Ellis Island.* 1922. Oil on panel. 14 × 18 inches. The National Museum of Women in the Arts, Washington, DC. Gift of Jacques S. Zinman.

Study each painting to find the following elements of rhythm.

✓ Which work has colors that are repeated?

✓ Find the shapes that are repeated.

✓ How are textures used in each artwork?

SEEING LIKE AN ARTIST
Look around the room. Find objects that are repeated.

Using Rhythm

We hear rhythm when sounds such as water dripping and hands clapping are repeated over and over. Rhythm can also be seen. Several children walking in line is an example of rhythm that can be seen. In artwork, shapes are repeated to create rhythm.

Visual rhythm is the feeling of movement created when artists repeat colors, shapes, lines, and textures. Your eyes move along their artwork, following the parts that are repeated. Each shape or object that is repeated is called a **motif**. In *Water Lilies,* the lily is a motif.

Random rhythm is created when a motif is repeated but in no particular order. For example, if you dropped a handful of crayons onto the floor, they would land pointing in all directions. This would show random rhythm.

Crayons lined up in their box are in a particular order. This shows **regular rhythm**.

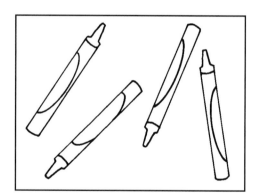
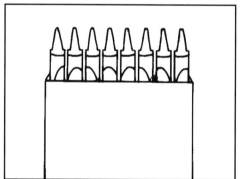

Practice

Demonstrate random rhythm. Use colored paper.

1. Cut a sheet of colored paper into many small pieces of the same shape.

2. Sprinkle the pieces on a large piece of colored paper. Try this several times.

Decide What is the motif in each design? In what order did the shapes land? Is the space between them always the same?

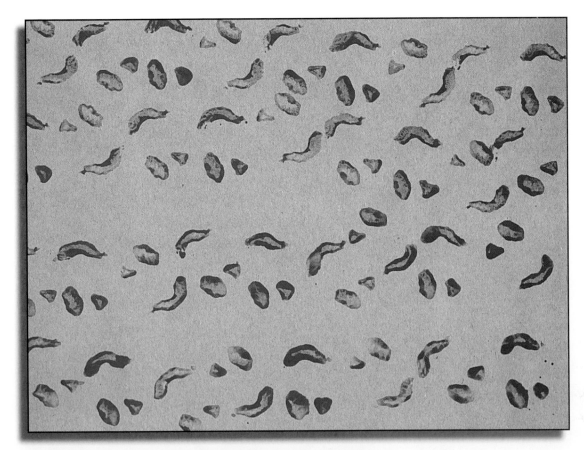

Sonnie Kroen. Age 8. *Kitchen Wallpaper.* Tempera paint.

How did this student artist create random rhythm?

Create

How can you use random rhythm to make wrapping paper? Design wrapping paper using random rhythm.

1. Think about a motif for your design. Make several sketches and choose your favorite.

2. Make a stamp of your design using half of a potato and a grapefruit spoon. Use random rhythm to print your motif on paper.

Describe What is your motif?

Analyze How did you create random rhythm? Can you clap out the rhythm of the motif with your hands?

Interpret Is the rhythm you used more like the one in Monet's painting or Walter's? How can you tell?

Decide Were you successful in creating a regular rhythm?

Regular Rhythm

Artists use regular rhythm to create a feeling
of movement and order in their artwork.

Mrs. Andy G. Byler. (American). *Double Wedding Ring Quilt*. c. 1930–1940. Cotton,
wool, linen, and rayon. $84 \times 66\frac{1}{6}$ inches. From the permanent collection of the
Museum of American Folk Art, New York, New York. Gift of Mrs. Andy G. Byler.

Look at the textile art on these pages. The *Double
Wedding Ring Quilt* was made by sewing
colorful scraps of cloth together with decorative
stitches. The Ottoman floor covering was woven in
the late 1500s, 350 years before the quilt. Regular
rhythm was used in the design of both pieces.

Artist unknown.
(Turkish). *Floor Covering* (Detail). Second half of sixteenth century. 16 feet 1 inch × 8 feet $9\frac{1}{2}$ inches. Velvet. Photograph © 1996 Detroit Institute of Arts, Gift of Edsel B. Ford, Detroit, Michigan.

Examine both textiles to find examples of regular rhythm.

- Find the shapes that are repeated over and over again. About how much space is between them?

- Which colors are repeated?

- Find negative or empty spaces that have been repeated. Find negative spaces that are about the same size and shape.

SEEING LIKE AN ARTIST

Look at clothes and other fabrics in your classroom. Find repeated shapes, lines, colors, or textures in them that are spaced evenly apart.

Lesson 5

153

Using Regular Rhythm

Regular rhythm is visual rhythm that is created by repeating the same motif with equal amounts of space in between. Regular rhythm is used to arrange things in an orderly way. Boxes and cans are usually placed in neat rows on shelves in grocery stores. This makes it easier to find what you are looking for. Parking spaces are arranged in regular rhythms, too. What would happen if people parked their cars wherever they wanted?

Artists sometimes use regular rhythm in their work, as well. Regular rhythm helps to organize motifs. A **motif** is a shape or an object that is repeated. For example, architects use regular rhythm to arrange windows in tall buildings.

Look at the drawing below. Name the motif. Why is it an example of regular rhythm?

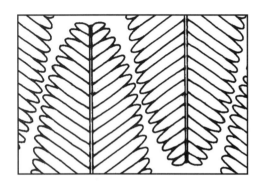

Practice

Illustrate regular rhythm. Use pencil or a marker in one color.

1. Fold a sheet of paper into six equal boxes. In the middle of the first box, draw a large geometric shape. Or you can write large and print a letter of the alphabet.

2. Draw exactly the same motif in each of the other boxes to create regular rhythm. Put equal amounts of space in between each letter or shape.

Decide Does the motif look the same in each box? Are there equal amounts of space between each one?

Fidel Gomez. Age 8. Construction paper.

What could you add to this student artist's design so that the design would still show regular rhythm?

Create

What objects would you choose to design a quilt? Design a quilt to illustrate regular rhythm.

1. Think about objects like those you see in nature. Select a few and make a rough sketch of each. Choose one as a motif.

2. Draw an outline of the object on stiff paper and cut it out. On colored paper, trace your motif six times. Cut out the shapes.

3. Fold a large sheet of paper into six boxes. Open it up. Glue a shape into each box. Remember to use equal amounts of space between the shapes.

4. Use colored scraps to add details to your motif in every other box.

Describe What object did you use for your motif? What colors did you repeat?

Analyze How did you create regular rhythm?

Interpret Explain what this motif means to you. Did repeating the motif change its meaning or the feeling of it? In what ways?

Decide If you could redo this collage, what parts would you change?

Alternating Rhythm

Artists use alternating rhythm in their artwork
to create movement and interest.

Henri Matisse. (French).
Purple Robe and Anemones.
1937. Oil on canvas. 73.1 ×
60.3 cm. The Baltimore
Museum of Art: The Cone
Collection, formed by Dr.
Claribel Cone and Miss Etta
Cone of Baltimore, Maryland.
© 1998 Succession H. Matisse,
Paris/Artists Rights Society
(ARS), New York.

Look at the artwork on these pages. *Purple Robe and Anemones* was painted by Henri Matisse. The deerhide *Parasol* was decorated with quills and beads. It was created in the early 1900s in the eastern Sioux style. Both artists have used alternating rhythm to design their artwork.

Artist unknown. Teton Lakota. (United States). *Parasol.*
Buckskin, quilled and beaded. $25\frac{1}{4} \times 23$ inches. Courtesy of the
Smithsonian National Museum of the American Indian, NY.
George H. Bingenheimer Collection. Photo by David Heald.

Search for the alternating rhythms in both works
of art.

☑ Find the motifs in each artwork. Which has more than
one motif?

☑ In which piece is the alternating rhythm harder to find?

☑ Find the artwork in which the motifs take turns
repeating.

☑ Which rhythm seems faster to you? Which seems
calmer? What other words describe the way these
rhythms feel?

SEEING LIKE AN ARTIST

Look at the designs in
the clothes your
classmates are
wearing. Find
examples of
alternating rhythm.

Using Alternating Rhythm

Alternating rhythm is a visual rhythm that can be created in different ways. It can be created by using two repeated motifs that alternate within a line. The motifs can also repeat in every other line.

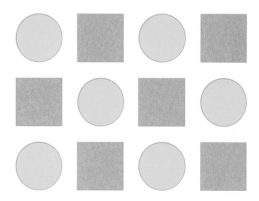

Another way to create rhythm is to use one motif and change its position to make a different alternating rhythm.

Practice

Role-play alternating rhythm in small groups.

1. Use your imagination to create an alternating rhythm with your group. Simple shapes will work best.

2. Try different ways to create alternating rhythm.

Decide What kinds of alternating rhythm did you show?

Teresa Diaz. Age 8. Tempera.

How did this student artist create alternating rhythm?

Create

How can you use alternating rhythm to show action figures? Design a mural featuring alternating rhythm.

1. Think about how you would look doing your favorite action activity. Make several sketches. Choose your best one.

2. Draw a self-portrait action outline, filling a piece of cardboard. Glue pieces of yarn around the outer edges and all other important lines.

3. Choose a partner and print a small mural using alternating rhythm.

Describe How did you create your action figure print? List the steps you used to create your mural.

Analyze How did you and your partner create alternating rhythm?

Interpret What action did you want your figures to show? Do they?

Decide What did you like best about making this mural?

Lesson 6

Texture and Rhythm in Music and Dance

"Voice/Dance": Tandy Beal and Bobby McFerrin.

have you ever done your own dance to music? You made up the movements as you went along. That's what a dancer and a musician do. One person sets out an idea and the other responds. They bounce ideas back and forth. In the picture, a musician is using his voice to respond to a dancer's moves. Together they create rhythm with movements and sounds.

What To Do

Make up movement in response to sounds.

Materials
✓ a drum or other musical instrument

1. Stand with your back to a drummer. He or she will beat a series of sounds with silences in between. When the drum is hit, respond with a quick, strong movement. Move in a different way each time.

2. Respond quickly to the sound. Move the moment you hear it. Move in a way that shows the rhythm or quality of the sound.

3. Next, experiment with sounds of the voice. These sounds could be yawning, coughing, sneezing, shushing, sighing, and whispering. Make a movement that catches the feeling and rhythm of the sound.

Describe Tell how you responded to the sounds.

Analyze Explain how you expressed rhythm.

Interpret What kinds of feelings or moods did you create?

Decide Which did you like better—making the sounds or the movements? Which was easier? Why?

Extra Credit

Work with a partner. Take turns creating the sounds and responding in movements. Perform for others.

Texture and Rhythm

Reviewing Main Ideas

The lessons and activities in this unit cover the techniques that artists use to create texture and rhythm.

1. **Texture** is the way the surface of an object feels or *looks* as if it would feel if you could touch it.

   • **Tactile texture** is the way the surface of an object *actually feels* when it is touched. *Appliqué* is an art form which creates tactile texture, by attaching cutout fabrics to a larger surface.

   • **Visual texture** is texture you see with your eyes.

2. **Visual rhythm** is the feeling of movement created by artists repeating colors, shapes, lines, and textures.

Tommye Scanlin. (American). *Blackeyed Susans.* Tapestry. 63 × 37 inches. Courtesy of Tommye Scanlin.

- **Random rhythm** is created when a motif is repeated in no particular order.
- **Regular rhythm** is created by repeating a motif with equal amounts of space in between.
3. **Alternating rhythm** is created by changing a motif every other time it appears or by taking turns repeating more than one motif.

Summing Up

Look at the weaving *Blackeyed Susans* by Tommye Scanlin. The artist used some of the techniques you learned about in this unit to create texture and rhythm.

- What kind of texture does the weaving have?
- What kind of rhythm do you see in the leaves and in the petals of the flowers?

By using techniques to create texture and rhythm, artists can create works of art that show how things feel and move.

Careers in Art
Weaver

Tommye Scanlin is a weaver who lives in Georgia. Weaving probably began when people twisted twigs and reeds together to make huts. Today, many artists, like Tommye Scanlin, use a loom and a variety of textured fibers to weave their own cloth. Many weavers study this craft in college. Scanlin taught herself how to weave by reading books. She creates her tapestry weavings on her own harness loom. She is a member of the Southern Highland Handicraft Guild. This is a group of craftspeople who sell their work in guild shops, hold exhibits, and bring people together to share ideas about handicrafts.

Tommye Scanlin, weaver

An Introduction to
Harmony, Variety, and Unity

Artists create harmony, variety, and unity in their artwork.

Frederic Remington. (American). *Mountain Man,* 1903. Bronze. The Carleton Collection.

Artists use **harmony** to make works of art look pleasing or peaceful.

• Where do you see shapes in *Mountain Man* that are similar?

• Which textures do you see more than once?

Some artists use **variety** to create interest.

• Describe at least two different textures you see.

• Describe some of these objects you see.

Harmony and variety create a feeling of **unity** in artwork.

• What unifies the sculpture?

Artist Profile

Frederic Remington
1861–1909

Self-Portrait on a Horse.

Frederic Remington was born in Canton, New York, on October 1, 1861. As a young boy, he loved to draw Native Americans, cowboys, soldiers, and horses. When he was 19 years old, he left college and traveled west. He spent four years as a cowboy and a rancher and sketched everything he saw. His artwork focuses on the American West.

Frederic Remington and other artists use harmony and variety to help them create unity in their artwork. In this unit you will learn and practice techniques for creating harmony and variety and learn how harmony and variety create a feeling of unity. You will study:

• Harmony   • Variety   • Unity

Harmony

**Artists create harmony to make a work
of art look pleasing or peaceful.**

Artist unknown. (Japan). Middle Jomon
period. *Jar.* c. 3000–2000 B.C. Earthenware
clay with applied, incised, and cord-marked
decoration. $27\frac{1}{2}$ inches. The Metropolitan
Museum of Art, New York, New York. The
Harry G. C. Packard Collection of Asian Art,
Gift of Harry G. C. Packard and Purchase,
Fletcher, Rogers, Harris Brisbane, Dick and
Louis V. Bell Funds, Joseph Pulitzer. Bequest
and the Annenberg Fund, Inc. Gift 1975.

Compare the ceramic containers shown on
these pages. The *Jar* was created in Japan
more than 4,000 years ago. The *Pottery Vessels*
were crafted by Nancy Youngblood Lugo in the
1990s. All the containers were made with clay.
Both works contain repeated lines and textures that
create harmony.

Nancy Youngblood Lugo. Pueblo (United States). *Pottery Vessels.* c. 1980–1985. Pottery. $4\frac{1}{2} \times 6$ inches in diameter. Courtesy Nancy Youngblood Lugo, © Jerry Jacka Photography.

Look closely at each ceramic piece to find examples of visual harmony.

✓ Look for shapes that are repeated.

✓ Find the textures that are repeated.

✓ Locate one of the **motifs** in each piece.

✓ Where do you see lines that are repeated?

SEEING LIKE AN ARTIST

Find a work of art in this book that seems peaceful to you. Which shapes, lines, or colors are repeated in it?

Using Harmony

Harmony is the peaceful look made when related elements of art are put together. Visual artists create harmony in many ways.

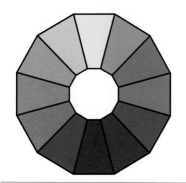

Harmony can be created with **colors** that are related on the color wheel.

Harmony can be created with similar **shapes**.

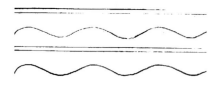

Harmony can be created with **repeated** lines, colors, shapes, textures, and objects.

Practice

Create harmony with color, shape, and repetition. Use markers or crayons.

1. Fold a sheet of paper into three parts. In the first part, draw a simple shape. Color it with three related colors.

2. In the second part, draw a geometric shape. Repeat the shape in different sizes until this part is filled.

3. In the last part, draw rows of repeating lines and shapes.

Decide Which part looks the most peaceful to you? Why?

What could be kept in this student artist's clay container?

Molly McCloskey. Age 8. *Star.* Clay.

Create

What would you keep in a clay container? Build a clay slab container designed with a texture to show harmony.

1. Think about textures you could add to your container. Gather objects that you could use to create texture.

2. Roll out a large slab of clay. Look at the textures each object makes on clay. Choose one.

3. Cut out a square from stiff paper, lay it on the clay, and cut around it. This will be your base.

4. Press your objects into the remaining clay slab until it is covered with texture. Trace the paper square and cut out four more pieces for the container's sides. Use proper joining techniques to assemble your container.

Describe What object did you use to create your textures?

Analyze Which elements did you repeat?

Interpret What does the texture you made remind you of?

Decide Does the container show harmony? Is there anything you would like to add or change to make it look more pleasing?

Variety

Artists use variety to create interest in their artwork.

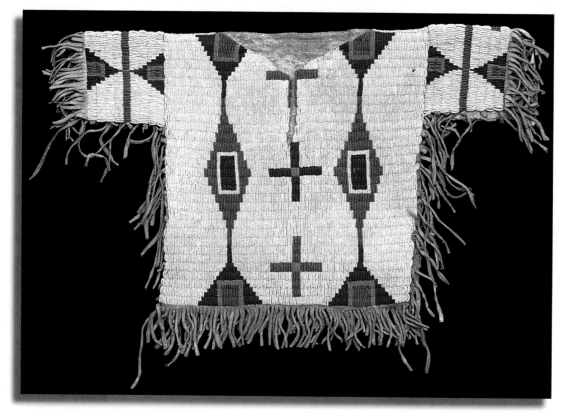

Artist unknown. Northern Cheyenne or Teton Dakota (United States). *Child's Beaded Shirt*. c. 1865. Buffalo hide, glass seed beads. 33.5 × 58.5 cm. Courtesy of the Dallas Museum of Art, Textile Purchase Fund.

Look at the **textile art** on these pages. A Central Plains woman made the *Child's Beaded Shirt* around 1865. It is decorated with a variety of textures, colors, and materials. The Navajo artist Isabel John created *Pictorial Tapestry* more than 100 years later with a variety of shapes and colors. Both artists used variety in their designs to create interest.

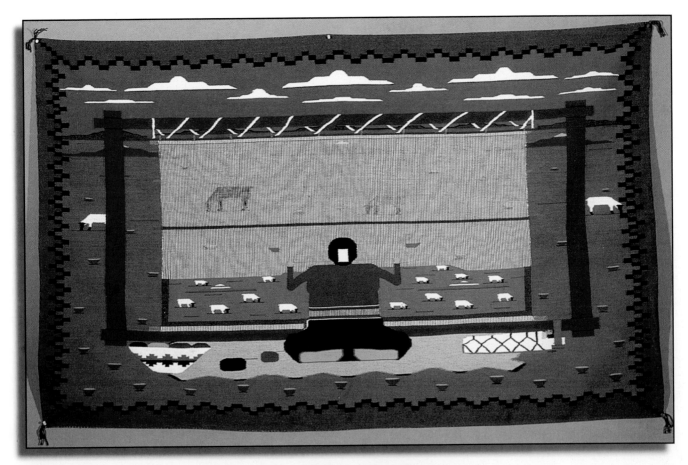

Isabel John. Navajo (United States). *Pictorial Tapestry.* Mid 1980s.
Wool, commercial, and natural dyes. 44 × 77 $\frac{1}{2}$ inches. Collection of the
Birmingham Museum of Art, Birmingham, Alabama. Museum purchase in
memory of Richard Kenneth McRae, with funds from family and friends.

Study both works of art to find examples of variety.

- ☑ Find different geometric and free-form shapes in the same artwork.

- ☑ Find shapes of different sizes in each piece.

- ☑ Locate places where you see different textures.

- ☑ Which work of art seems to have more variety?

SEEING LIKE AN ARTIST

Choose an element of art such as line, color, shape, or texture. How many different varieties can you find in your classroom?

Using Variety

Variety is using different lines, shapes, colors, and textures to make a work of art interesting.

Too much of the same color, line, or shape in an artwork can be boring, but adding something different or unexpected can break up the repetition. Using a variety of colors or lines can give people more to think about.

See if you can tell what has been changed to add variety to each of the designs below.

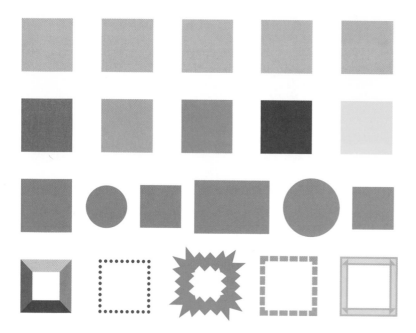

Practice

Create a design that has variety. Use pencil and one other medium, if you like.

1. Draw a geometric or free-form shape on your paper with a pencil. Repeat the shape, the same size, until your paper is filled.

2. Add a different element to your design to create variety. For example, you might add different colors, lines, or textures.

Decide What did you do to add variety to your design? Did the variety make the design more interesting?

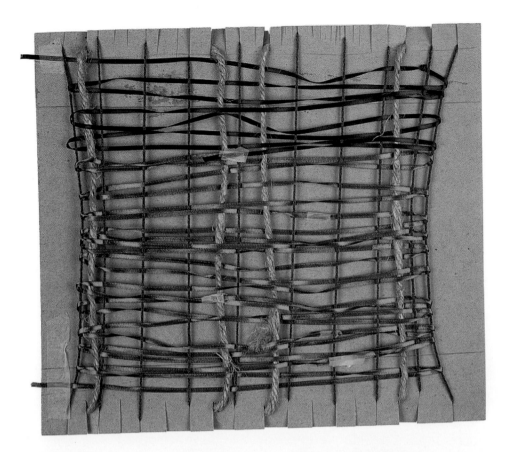

Aaron Romaro. Age 8. *Varied Lines.* Yarn, ribbon, and cardboard.

What textures did this student artist use in his weaving?

Create

What different ways can you use a weaving? Make a weaving with a variety of colors and textures.

1. Think about how you will use your weaving. Select a variety of ribbons, natural fibers, and yarn for your weaving.

2. Cut out a piece of cardboard, and notch it on the top and the bottom. Then, string the warp thread on it.

3. Weave your fibers to create variety.

Describe What colors and textures did you use in your weaving?

Analyze Which colors and textures did you repeat? Where did you create variety?

Interpret How would the interest of your weaving change if you had used only one color and one texture?

Decide If you could add other colors and textures, what would you choose?

Harmony and Variety

Artists create harmony with similar shapes, lines, or textures. They introduce variety by changing some of these elements.

Artist unknown. (Babylonia). *Ishtar Gate.* c. 605–562 B.C. State Museum, Berlin, Germany. Erich Lessing/Art Resource, NY.

Look at the mosaics on these pages. *Ishtar Gate* was designed and created in Babylonia about 2,500 years ago. The other work of art is a small part of a large mosaic in a church. Both mosaics have harmony and variety.

Artist unknown. (Italy). *Ravenna Apse Mosaic (Detail)*. A.D. 549. The Church of Saint Apollinaris, Ravenna, Italy. Scala/Art Resource, New York.

Study each mosaic to find the following examples of harmony and variety.

- ✓ Find colors that are related to each other.

- ✓ Locate the shapes that are repeated all over.

- ✓ Find geometric shapes next to free-form shapes.

- ✓ Locate colors that are different from each other.

SEEING LIKE AN ARTIST
Look through this book and find an artwork that shows harmony and variety together in the same piece.

Lesson 3

Using Harmony and Variety in Mosaics

A **mosaic** is a picture made by setting small pieces of colored tile, glass, or stone side by side.

Harmony can be created in mosaics by using similar shapes throughout the design. This sometimes creates a feeling of peacefulness.

Variety can also be found in mosaics through the use of different materials, such as glass, marble, tile, stone, gold, and shell. Using a variety of lines, shapes, colors, and textures also adds interest.

The art of mosaic is still used today to decorate religious and public buildings.

Practice

Illustrate harmony in a paper mosaic. Use construction paper.

Decide How did you create harmony?

1. Draw the large outline of an object on a sheet of paper.

2. Choose construction paper in two related colors. Tear the paper into strips. Tear the strips into rectangles and triangles to make tiles.

3. Lay the pieces on the drawing until it is filled. Leave small spaces between the pieces.

How did this student artist create variety and harmony in an animal mosaic?

Jack Maloy. Age 8. *Owl.* Cut paper.

Create

What animal shape would make an interesting mosaic? Create a paper mosaic to show harmony and variety.

1. Think about the shapes of different animals. Choose one and draw its shape with chalk on black paper.

2. Make mosaic pieces by cutting colored paper into strips. Cut the strips into the shapes you want to use. Fill the outline with warm colors and a variety of small shapes. Glue them down.

3. Next, cut small pieces of cool-colored construction paper. Glue them onto the background areas around your animal.

Describe What colors did you use for your mosaic? Describe the shapes of the mosaic pieces.

Analyze Did you create variety? Did you create harmony?

Interpret Where would be the best place in town to hang your class's mosaics? Explain.

Decide How did you balance harmony and variety in your mosaic?

Unity

Artists balance harmony and variety
to create unity in a work of art.

Artist unknown. (United States). *Duncan House Bedroom*. c. 1805. Bed-sitting room.
Haverhill, Massachusetts. The Metropolitan Museum of Art, New York, New York.

Look at the rooms on these pages. The *Duncan House Bedroom* was designed in 1805 for a private home in Massachusetts. *Bedroom (cubiculum nocturnum)* is a Roman burial chamber. It was built and decorated more than 2,000 years ago. Both rooms were designed and decorated to create a feeling of unity. The variety of materials and objects is balanced by the harmony of colors and shapes.

Artist unknown. (Roman). *Bedroom (cubiculum nocturnum)*.
40–30 B.C. Fresco on lime plaster. 8 feet $8\frac{1}{2}$ inches × 19 feet $1\frac{7}{8}$ inches × 10 feet $11\frac{1}{2}$ inches.
The Metropolitan Museum of Art, New York,
New York. Rogers Fund, 1903. Photograph by Shecter Lee.

Study both rooms to find examples of unity.

☑ Find related shapes. Where are they repeated?

☑ Find the two main colors in each room. Where do you see them repeated?

☑ Do you see a variety of textures? Describe them.

☑ Locate objects that are repeated.

☑ Does one room seem to have more variety than the other? Does one have more harmony? How can you tell?

Lesson 4

Using Unity

Unity is the "invisible glue" that makes different parts look as if they belong together. It helps you see a work of art as a whole instead of as separate parts. Artists have different ways of creating unity. One way is to balance harmony and variety. This gives them equal weight.

Harmony is created by using similar shapes or related colors to give a work the feeling of oneness or belonging.

Variety is created by using different lines, shapes, colors, and textures to give a work the feeling of oneness or belonging.

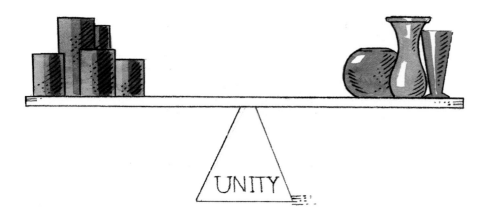

Simplicity is another way to create unity. Sometimes artists make everything in a work one color, texture, or shape to create simplicity.

Practice

Create and color a design that illustrates unity. Use colored pencils.

1. Draw a variety of geometric and free-form shapes to create a design.

2. Color the shapes with warm colors.

3. Choose a cool color to fill the spaces between and around the shapes.

Decide How did you create unity in your design?

Yori Lai. Age 8. Crayon.

What is the center of interest in this student artist's dream room?

Create

What would be the perfect room for you? Design a dream room that illustrates unity.

1. Think about what your dream room would look like. Make several sketches of it. Choose one and draw it with crayon.

2. Create harmony in your drawing by repeating colors that are related. Use a contrasting color to create a center of interest.

3. To create unity, cover the whole paper with one color of watercolor.

Describe What objects did you draw in your room? What colors did you use?

Analyze Where did you create harmony in the room? Where did you add variety? How did you give your drawing a feeling of unity?

Interpret Does your drawing look like your dream room? Explain.

Decide What do you like best about this room?

Lesson 4

Unity, Repetition, and Grouping

Artists use repetition and grouping to create unity in a work of art.

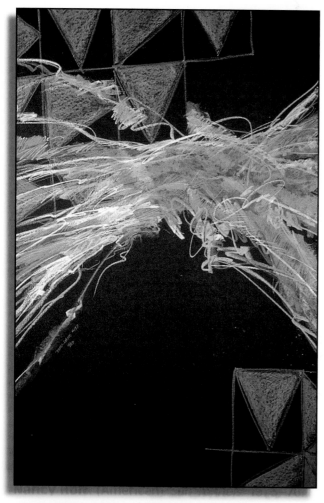

Willis Bing Davis. (American). *Ancestral Spirit Dance Series.*
1990. Oil pastel. 60 × 40 inches. Courtesy of Willis Bing Davis.

Look at the paintings on these pages. Henri Matisse painted *Woman in Blue* in France. About 50 years later, Willis Bing Davis painted *Ancestral Spirit Dance Series*, an abstract design based on memories of African dancers. Both artists have created unity to give their work a feeling of wholeness.

Henri Matisse. (French). *Woman in Blue.* 1937. Oil on canvas. $36\frac{1}{2} \times 29$ inches. Philadelphia Museum of Art, Philadelphia, Pennsylvania. Gift of Mrs. John Wintersteen/© 1998 Succession H. Matisse, Paris/Artists Rights Society (ARS), New York.

Study both artworks to find examples of unity.

✓ Where do you see geometric shapes combined with wild zigzag lines?

✓ Name the colors in each work. How many are there in each?

✓ Locate the thin lines repeated throughout *Woman in Blue.*

SEEING LIKE AN ARTIST
Look outdoors. Find objects in nature that are surrounded by a single color.

Using Unity

Unity is the feeling of wholeness in a work of art. You have already seen how harmony and variety can create unity in a work of art.

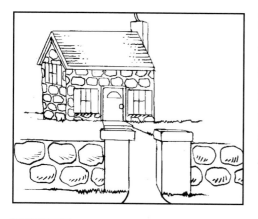

Repetition is another way artists show that different parts of a work belong together. An architect, for example, might repeat the colors and textures found in the environment on the outside of the house.

Seashells arranged on a beach are a good example of unity. They are usually different shapes and sizes, but the sand in the background unifies them.

Practice

Illustrate unity. Use pencil and crayon.

1. Draw a large free-form shape. Fill it with a variety of smaller geometric shapes.

2. Use pencil to darken the spaces between the geometric shapes. Use crayon to color the whole area outside the free-form shape one color.

Decide How did you create unity in your design?

How does this student artist show unity in her design?

Toni Thompson. Age 8. *Kingdom.* Crayon and school acrylics.

Create

How can you use creatures to show unity? Create a crayon engraving.

1. Think about insects and reptiles with interesting shapes. Use crayons to cover a sheet of paper with many different colors. Then, paint the whole surface with thinned black ink until you can't see the color.

2. While the ink is drying, sketch a few real or imaginary reptiles and insects on scratch paper. Choose some to draw.

3. Engrave the creatures in different shapes and sizes by scratching lines and line patterns in the black background with the pointed end of a paper clip. This is called **crayon engraving.** Add detail and texture.

Describe What creatures did you draw? What colors did you use? Describe your lines.

Analyze How did you create unity in your engraving? What happened when you engraved your lines?

Interpret How would the mood of your picture change if you had not covered the surface with black ink?

Decide Can you think of another theme to use for this art project?

Unity in Handmade Books

Artists unify pages when they make books and their covers.

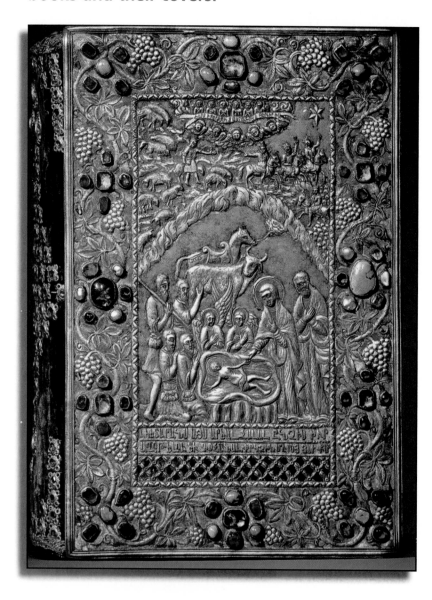

Artist unknown. (Armenia). *Cover of Armenian Book.* Thirteenth century. Carved and hammered silver, gilded and enameled, and set with jewels, rubricated vellum. $10\frac{1}{4} \times 7\frac{3}{8}$ inches. The Metropolitan Museum of Art, New York, New York. Gift of Mrs. Edward S. Harkness, 1916.

Look at the book covers on these pages. The *Cover of Armenian Book* is made from precious metal and decorated with a variety of gemstones. Kathryn Gough created *Book Cover* in the 1990s. She painted make-believe gemstones and precious metal. The covers unify the pages of these books. Unity is also an important part of the designs on the covers.

Kathryn Gough. (American). *Book Cover,* 1995. Oil on paper. 5 × 6 inches. Hudak private collection.

Study both book covers to find examples of unity.

- ✓ Find shapes that are similar.

- ✓ Where do you see the same motif repeated?

- ✓ Name the colors in each. How many are there?

- ✓ Where do you see a variety of shapes grouped closely together?

- ✓ Locate the negative spaces painted or dyed one color.

- ✓ Find shapes and colors that are inside a larger shape.

SEEING LIKE AN ARTIST
Look at books in your classroom. What clues on the covers hint at what is inside?

Using Bookmaking to Show Unity

Bookmaking is the art of binding or tying pages together inside a cover. It is an example of **unity,** or wholeness. A cover design unifies the contents of a book by holding the pages together.

Artists have been making books by hand for thousands of years. They create books in many different ways using a variety of materials.

Practice

Create an alphabet book for a kindergarten class. Use crayon.

1. Each student can illustrate a letter, adding objects that begin with the letter.

2. Place all the letters inside a folded paper to make a book.

3. Add a title and decorate the cover.

Decide How did you unify the drawings?

How did this student artist create unity?

Leanne Jewel. Age 8. Markers.

Create

What are the most important things about you? Show unity in a book about yourself.

1. Think about things you like to do and things that are important to you.

2. Put two sheets of paper together and fold them in half to make the pages of a book. Draw pictures that tell about you.

3. Fold a sheet of paper in half to make a cover. Write your name and the title of your book. Then, illustrate the front. Slide your pages inside and staple.

Describe What things describe you?

Analyze How did you create unity in your book?

Interpret Why did you choose the title?

Decide If you could redo some of the pages, which ones would you change? Why?

Lesson 6

Harmony, Variety, and Unity in Theater

In the Heart of the Beast Puppet and Mask Theatre: *On the Day You Were Born.*

On the Day You Were Born is a book by Debra Frasier. It tells about events in nature that happen on the day a child enters the world. A play based on the book uses puppets, paintings, poems, and music to celebrate nature. The play welcomes each new member of the human family into the world.

What To Do

Use your body and voice to express information about science and nature.

Materials
- ✔ poems and stories
- ✔ recordings of music

1. List some natural events.

2. Take each event and add an action word to it. Example: spinning Earth.

3. Work in a small group. Choose one event to explore through sound and movement. Think of different ways to show each event. You can combine dance, music, poems, and stories.

4. Think of an exciting way to begin. Next, plan some actions with sounds of talking or music to go with them. Then, decide on the end. Use harmony and variety to create balance in your scene.

5. Perform your scene for the class.

Describe Tell how your group thought up ideas and made decisions.

Analyze Explain how you used harmony, variety, and unity to dramatize your idea.

Interpret What is the mood of your scene?

Decide Do you think you succeeded in creating movements and sounds to express your ideas?

Extra Credit ·

Select another natural event. Use the same sound and motion techniques to work out a new scene. Work alone or with a partner. Perform your scene for others.

Theater

Harmony, Variety, and Unity

Reviewing Main Ideas

The lessons and activities in this unit cover the techniques that artists use to create harmony, variety, and unity.

1. **Harmony** is the peaceful look made when related elements of art are put together. Harmony can be created by using related colors, shapes, and repetition of elements.

2. **Variety** is created when different lines, shapes, colors, and textures are used to make a work of art interesting.

   • *Repetition* is one way artists create unity.

   • *Bookmaking,* binding pages together inside a cover, also creates unity.

3. *Mosaics* are pictures made by setting small pieces of colored tile, glass, or stone side by side. Harmony can be created in mosaics by using similar shapes. Variety can be created by using different materials.

4. **Unity** is a feeling of oneness in a work of art. Unity can be created by balancing harmony and variety.

Auguste Rodin. *The Thinker,* 1880. Bronze. $51\frac{1}{4} \times 55\frac{1}{4}$ inches. The Rodin Museum, Philadelphia: Gift of Jules E. Mastbaum.

Summing Up

The *Thinker* is a sculpture by Auguste Rodin. In this sculpture, Rodin used the principles of harmony, variety, and unity covered in this unit.

- Which lines do you see more than once in this sculpture?
- How many different kinds of textures can you find in this sculpture?
- What color is the sculpture?

Harmony, variety, and unity are important principles in art. By using techniques to create harmony, variety, and unity, artists can create a work of art that is pleasing, interesting, and has a feeling of oneness.

Let's Visit a Museum

The Philadelphia Museum of Art was established in Philadelphia, Pennsylvania, in 1875. There are over 300,000 objects in the museum's collection. The Asian collection has artwork dating from 500 B.C. to the present. The European collections have sculpture, stained glass, and paintings. The American collections have paintings, furniture, silver, and Pennsylvania German art. In addition, the museum offers many programs for people of all ages. These include school tours, workshops, and performances for families.

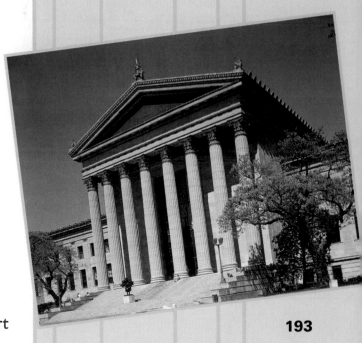

The Philadelphia Museum of Art

193

More About...
Technique Tips

Pencil

With the side of your pencil lead, press harder and shade over areas more than once for darker values. With a pencil, you can add form to your objects by shading.

Colored Pencil

You can blend colors with colored pencils.
Color with the lighter color first.
Gently color over it with the darker
color until you have the effect you want.

Shadows or darker values can be created
by blending complementary colors.

More About...
Technique Tips

Crayon

Crayons can be used to make thin lines or thick lines. You can use both ends of the crayon.

Crayons can also be used to make small or large dots. You can use both ends of the crayon.

Use either the side of the point or the side of the whole crayon to color large spaces.

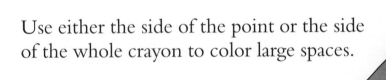

You can also blend different colors to create the hues you want. Color with the lighter color first. Gently color over it with the darker color until you have the effect you want.

Marker

Marker can be used to make either sketches or finished drawings.
Use the point of a marker to make thin lines and small dots.

The side of the tip makes thick lines.

Always replace the cap so the marker doesn't dry out.

Technique Tips

Oil Pastels

Oil pastels can be used like crayons. When you press down hard with oil pastels, your pictures will look painted. Oil pastels are soft and can break easily. These pieces are still usable. Oil pastels can be messy. Wash your hands with soap and water after using them.

Colors can be mixed or blended by smearing them together with your finger or a tissue.

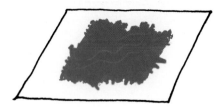

You can also use oil pastels to color over other media, such as tempera or crayon. Then, you can scratch through this covering to create a design.

Colored Chalk

Colored chalks can be used to make colorful, soft designs. Because they are soft, colored chalks break easily. These pieces are still usable.

You can make bolder colors by coloring over an area more than once.

You can also blend colors by using your finger and a soft tissue.

More About...
Technique Tips

Tempera

1. Fill water containers halfway. Dip your brush in water. Wipe your brush on the inside edge of the container. Then, blot it on a paper towel to get rid of extra water. Remember to clean your brush before using a new color.

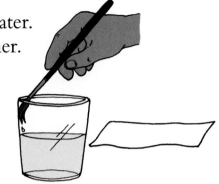

2. Always mix colors on a palette. Put some of each color that you want to mix on the palette. Add the darker color a little at a time to the lighter color.

3. To create lighter values, mix a little of the color or hue into white. To darken a value, add a tiny amount of black until you have the value you want.

4. Use a thin, pointed brush to paint thin lines and details. For thick lines or large areas, press firmly on the tip or use a wide brush.

5. Wash your brushes when you are done. Reshape the bristles. Store brushes with the bristles up.

Technique Tips

Watercolor

1. Fill water containers halfway. Dip your brush in water. Wipe your brush on the inside edge of the container. Then, blot it on a paper towel to get rid of extra water. With your brush, add a drop of water to each watercolor cake and stir. Remember to clean your brush whenever you change colors.

2. Always mix colors on a palette. Put some of each color that you want to mix on the palette. Add the darker color a little at a time to the lighter color.

3. To create lighter values, add more water. To darken a hue, add a tiny amount of black until you get the value you want.

4. Use a thin, pointed brush to paint thin lines and details. For thick lines or large areas, press firmly on the tip or use a wide brush.

5. For a softer look, tape your paper to the table with masking tape. Use a wide brush to add water to the paper, working in rows from top to bottom. Let the water soak in a little. Painting on wet paper will create a soft or fuzzy look. For sharper forms or edges, paint on dry paper. Use only a little water in your brush.

6. Wash your brushes when you are done. Reshape the bristles. Store brushes with the bristles up.

Technique Tips

Printmaking: Making Stamps

Various ways of making stamps for printmaking are listed below. You can cut either a positive or negative shape into most of these objects.

- Cut sponges into shapes.

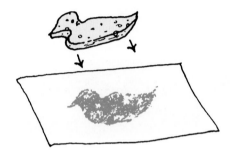

- Draw or sculpt a design on a flat piece of modeling clay. Use a pencil, a clay tool, the tip of a paperclip, or another object.

Technique Tips

Printmaking: Printing Stamps

1. Put a small amount of water-based printing ink or some paint onto a flat, solid surface. Roll a soft roller, called a brayer, back and forth in the ink until there is an even coating of paint on both the surface and the brayer.

2. Roll the brayer over the top of your stamp. The ink should cover the stamp evenly without going into the grooves of your design.

3. Apply your stamp carefully to your paper. You can rub the back of the paper with the side of your fist to make sure all parts of the stamp get printed. Then, peel the paper and stamp apart and check your print. If you wish to make several prints of your design, you should ink your stamp again as needed.

4. When you are finished, wash the brayer, surface, and stamp.

Technique Tips

Collage

In a collage, objects or pieces of paper, fabric, or other materials are attached to a surface to create a work of art. When planning your collage, consider such things as:

- Size of shapes and spaces

- Placement of shapes and spaces

- Color schemes

- Textures

Remember that the empty (negative) spaces are also part of your design. Plan a collage as you would plan a painting or drawing. Decide what shapes and objects you want to use. Arrange them on the paper. When you have made an arrangement you like, glue your shapes and objects to the paper.

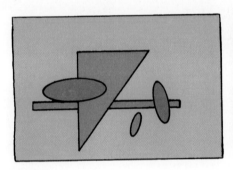 

More About...
Technique Tips

Papier-Mâché—Strip Method

The strip method of papier-mâché ("mashed paper") uses paper combined with paste. Often, papier-mâché is molded over a form that helps it keep its shape while it's drying.

1. Create a supporting form, if needed. Forms can be made from clay, wadded-up newspaper, cardboard boxes and tubes, balloons, wire, or other materials. Masking tape can be used to hold the form together.

2. Tear paper into strips. Either dip the strips into a thick mixture of paste or rub paste on the strips with your fingers. Use wide strips to cover wide forms. Use thin strips or small pieces to cover a small shape.

3. Apply five or six layers of strips. Lay each layer in a different direction. For example, lay the first layer vertically and the second horizontally. Smooth over all rough edges with your fingers. If you are going to leave the form in place, two or three layers of strips should be enough.

4. When it is dry, you can paint your sculpture.

More About...
Technique Tips

Clay

1. Pinch and pull clay into the desired shape.

2. To join two pieces of clay together:
   - *score,* or scratch, both pieces so they will stick together.
   - attach the pieces with some *slip,* which is watery clay
   - *squeeze* the two pieces together
   - *smooth* the edges

3. To carve a design out of clay, scratch or dig out your design with a paper clip or other tools.

4. To roll a slab of clay, press a ball of clay into a flat shape on a cloth-covered board. Place one 1/4" slat on each side of the clay. Use a roller to press the slab into an even thickness. With a straightened paper clip, trim the slab into the desired shape.

5. Wrap unfinished sculptures in plastic to keep them moist until you are finished.

More About...
Art Criticism

Horace Pippin. (American). *Victorian Parlor II.* 1945. Oil on canvas. $25\frac{1}{4} \times$ 30 inches. The Metropolitan Museum of Art, New York, Arthur H. Heam Fund, 1958.

Art Criticism

DESCRIBE

Make a list of everything you see in this painting.

ANALYZE

How has the artist used line, shape, color, value, space, and texture?

How has the artist used rhythm, balance, emphasis, variety, and harmony to organize this painting?

Horace Pippin. (American). *Victorian Parlor II.* 1945. Oil on canvas. $25\frac{1}{4} \times 30$ inches. The Metropolitan Museum of Art, New York, Arthur H. Heam Fund, 1958.

INTERPRET

What is the artist telling you about the people who live in this room?

DECIDE

Have you ever seen another work of art that looks like this painting?

Is it successful because it is realistic?

Is it successful because it is well-organized?

Is it successful because you have strong feelings when you study it?

LOOK

Horace Pippin. (American). *Victorian Parlor II.* 1945. Oil on canvas. $25\frac{1}{4} \times$ 30 inches. The Metropolitan Museum of Art, New York, Arthur H. Heam Fund, 1958.

LOOK AGAIN

Look at the work of art.

What sounds are in this work of art?

What smells are in this work of art?

If you could take parts away from the work of art, what would they be and why?

What happened just before and just after in this work of art?

Horace Pippin. (American). *Victorian Parlor II.* 1945. Oil on canvas. $25\frac{1}{4} \times 30$ inches. The Metropolitan Museum of Art, New York, Arthur H. Heam Fund, 1958.

LOOK INSIDE

Look at the work of art.

Describe the rest of this house. How many rooms are there and what is in each room?

Tell or write a story about this work of art with a beginning, a middle, and an end.

How would it feel to sit in one of those chairs?

LOOK OUTSIDE

Look at the work of art.

How is this like or different from your own life?

How would you change this work of art to be more like your life? What would the changes be? What would the artwork look like?

What does the artist want you to know or think about in this work of art?

Describe the people who visit this house.

What does the outside of this house look like? What kind of neighborhood is it in?

What will you remember about this work?

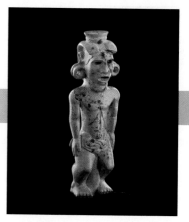

Artist unknown.
Adena Effigy Figure.
1000–300 B.C. United States.

Artist unknown.
Three Cows and One Horse.
15,000–13,000 B.C. France.

Artist unknown.
Statues from Abu Temple.
2700–2000 B.C. Iraq.

Artist unknown.
Tutankhamen Mask (side view).
C. 1340 B.C. Egypt.

Artist unknown.
Chuang.
1100 B.C. China.

Artist unknown.
Colossal Head.
1500–300 B.C. Mexico.

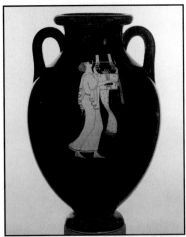

Artist unknown.
Woman Playing Harp.
(Detail from vase.) c. 490 B.C.

Artist unknown.
Parthenon.
448–432 B.C. Greece.

Artist unknown.
Stonehenge.
1800–1400 B.C. England.

More About...Art History

Artist unknown.
Shiva as Lord of the Dance.
1000. India.

Artist unknown.
Ravenna Apse Mosaic. (Detail).
A.D. 100. Italy.

Artist unknown.
The Pantheon.
A.D. 118–125. Italy.

Artist unknown.
Hagia Sophia.
A.D. 532–537. Turkey.

Artist unknown.
The Great Stupa (at Sanchi).
200–100 B.C. India.

Artist unknown.
Page from *The Book of Lindisfarne*.
Late 600s. England.

Artist unknown.
*Pagoda of the Temple
of the Six Banyan Trees.*
A.D. 537. China.

Artist unknown.
Stupa (at Borobudur).
800. Indonesia.

Artist unknown.
Great Mosque
(at Samarra).
648–852. Iraq.

More About...Art History

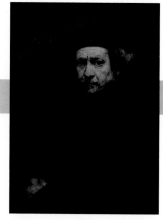

Rembrandt van Rijn.
Self-Portrait.
1660. The Netherlands.

Leonardo da Vinci.
Mona Lisa.
1503–1505. Italy.

Artist unknown.
Bayon Temple at Angkor Thom.
1100s–1200s. Cambodia.

Artist unknown.
Shrine Head. (Yorub).
1100–1300. Nigeria.

Torii Kiyotada.
Actor of the Ichikawa Clan.
1710–1740. Japan.

Artist unknown.
Chartres Cathedral.
1145–1220. France.

Thomas Jefferson.
Monticello.
1770–1784. United States.

Artist unknown.
Bayeux Tapestry. (Detail).
1070–1080. England.

Artist unknown.
Anasazi culture petroglyphs.
United States.

Artist unknown.
Taj Mahal.
1632–1648. India.

More About...Art History

More About...
Art History

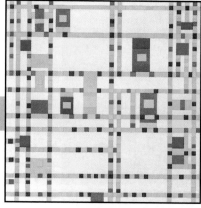

Piet Mondrian.
Broadway Boogie-Woogie.
1941. The Netherlands.

Claude Monet.
Impression, Sunrise.
1872. France.

Edgar Degas.
Little Dancer of Fourteen.
1880–1881. France.

Katsushika Hokusai.
The Great Wave off Kanagawa.
1831–1833. Japan.

Pablo Picasso.
Gertrude Stein.
1906. Spain.

Chuck Close.
Self-Portrait.
1987. United States.

Jackson Pollock.
Convergence.
1952. United States.

Maria Martínez.
Black on Black Pot.
1920. United States.

Alexander Calder.
Untitled Mobile.
1959. United States.

More About...Art History

Subject Matter

Artists create art about many subjects. *Subject matter* refers to the content of an artist's artwork. For example, the subject of a painting can be a vase of flowers or a self-portrait. This subject matter is easy to identify. The subject matter becomes more difficult to understand when the artwork stands for something beyond itself. Look at the artwork on these pages. Notice the different words used to identify different kinds of subject matter.

Still Life

Odilon Redon. *Bouquet of Flowers.* 1905. Pastel on paper. $31\frac{5}{8} \times 25\frac{1}{4}$ inches. Metropolitan Museum of Art, New York, Gift of Mrs. George B. Post, 1956.

More About...
Subject Matter

Landscape

Thomas Hart Benton. (American). *July Hay.* 1943.
Oil and egg tempera on composition board. $38 \times 26\frac{3}{4}$ inches.
Metropolitan Museum of Art, New York, George A. Heam Fund,
© 1998. T. H. Benton and R. P. Benton Testamentary Trusts/
Licensed by VAGA, New York, NY.

Subject Matter

Genre

Jean-Honoré Fragonard. (French). *A Young Girl Reading.*
c. 1776. National Gallery of Art,
Mellon Collection, Washington, D.C.

More About...
Subject Matter

Nonobjective

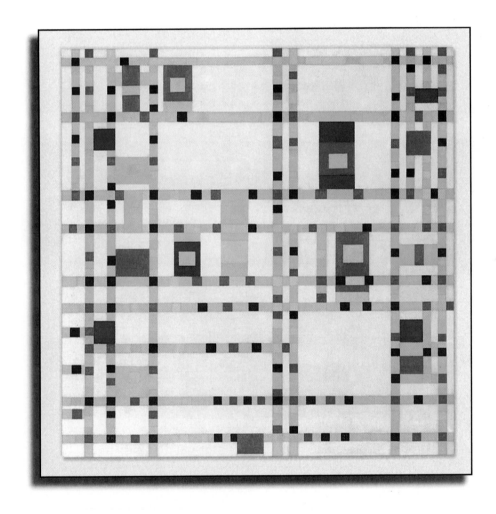

Piet Mondrian. (Dutch). *Broadway Boogie-Woogie.* 1942–43.
Oil on canvas. 50 × 50 inches. The Museum of Modern Art,
New York. Given anonymously. Photograph © 1998
The Museum of Modern Art, New York.

More About...
Subject Matter

Self-Portrait

Gerard Dou. (Dutch). *Self-Portrait.*
Oil on wood. $19\frac{1}{4} \times 15\frac{3}{8}$ inches.
Metropolitan Museum of Art, New York,
Bequest of Benjamin Altman, 1913.

Symbols

Childe Hassam. (American). *Avenue
of the Allies, Great Britain.* 1918.
Oil on canvas. $36 \times 28\frac{3}{8}$ inches.
Metropolitan Museum of Art, New
York, Bequest of Miss Adelaide
Milton de Groot (1876–1967) 1967.

A Story Shown as Symbols

Artist unknown. (English). *The Five Senses: Hearing.* (Detail).
c. 1650–1675. White satin embroidered in petit
point and enriched with seed pearls and coral.
Metropolitan Museum of Art, New York.

More About...
Still-Life Drawing

Everything you see is filled with lines and shapes you already know how to draw.

More About...
Still-Life Drawing

LOOK

Look carefully at the photograph of the still life.

- ☑ Find the square around the front edge of the red box.
- ☑ Find the circle that makes the edge of the basketball.
- ☑ Find the free-form shape that outlines the teddy bear.
- ☑ Find the horizontal lines on the front edge of the table.
- ☑ Find the diagonal lines on the edges of the sides of the table.
- ☑ Find the vertical lines on the edges of the four table legs. Notice that the back legs of the table appear shorter.

PRACTICE

Look for a table in your classroom. Find lines like the ones you see in the photograph. Practice drawing the table in your room.

More About...
Drawing People

People are made of free-form shapes. These shapes change depending upon what position a person is in.

More About...
Drawing People

LOOK

Look at the three people in the photograph. Notice the shape and size of heads, necks, torsos, arms, legs, hands, and feet. These are free-form shapes.

- ☑ How are the walking person's arms and legs bending?
- ☑ Where does the sitting person's body bend?
- ☑ The standing person's feet are pointing toward you. These are like vertical ovals.
- ☑ How is the shape of the person's head that's facing you different from the profile of the people facing sideways?

PRACTICE

Look at the people in your classroom. Can you find the same shapes in their heads as you see in the picture? Practice drawing a person facing you. Try to draw vertical oval shapes to make their feet look like they are pointing toward you.

More About...
Drawing Landscapes

When you look at a landscape, you can see that some
things are in front of or behind other things.

More About...
Drawing Landscapes

LOOK

Look at the landscape with the horses.

- ✓ Find the horse in the **foreground,** the front of the picture.
- ✓ Find the horse in the **background,** the back of the picture.

The one in the foreground is larger because it is closer. Things that are far away appear smaller. You cannot see part of the horse in the background because the tree and the other horse are in front of it, or **overlap** it.

PRACTICE

Practice overlapping. Draw a large square in front of a small circle. First, draw the large square. Place your pencil point on an edge of the square. Begin drawing part of a small circle. Stop your pencil when you bump back into the square.

Look around your classroom for objects that overlap. Practice drawing them.

Visual Index: Artworks Arranged in Time Order

Artist unknown
Jar
3000–2000 B.C.
page 166

Artist unknown
Portrait of a Boy
Second century
page 118

Artist unknown
Winged Genie
883–859 B.C.
page 93

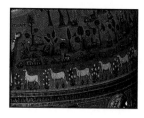

Artist unknown
*Ravenna Apse
Mosaic (Detail)*
A.D. 549
page 175

Artist unknown
Ishtar Gate
c. 605–562 B.C.
page 174

Artist unknown
Shirt Section
C. A.D. 600–1000
page 137

Artist unknown
*Bedroom (cubiculum
nocturnum)*
40–30 B.C.
page 178

Artist unknown
*Hats: Birds and
Geometric Patterns*
700–1000
page 50

Visual Index

Artist unknown
Jar
Twelfth century
page 107

Lorenzo Ghiberti
*The Meeting of
Solomon and Sheba:
The Gates of Paradise*
1425–1452
page 92

Artist unknown
*Cover of Armenian
Book*
Thirteenth century
page 186

Artist unknown
*Sleeveless Shirt
(two cats)*
c. 1438–1532
page 76

Artist unknown
Mihrab
1354
page 29

Wang Chao
*The Three Stars of
Happiness, Wealth,
and Longevity*
c. 1500
page 21

Visual Index

Artist unknown
Covered Jar
1522–1566
page 67

John Singleton Copley
Daniel Crommelin Verplanck
1771
page 36

Artist unknown
Floor Covering Detail
Second half of sixteenth century
page 153

Artist unknown
Symmetrical View of a Totem Pole
Nineteenth century
page 114

Hyacinthe Rigaud
Louis XV as a Child
1715
page 145

Artist unknown
Symmetrical View of a Totem Pole
Nineteenth century
page 115

Rachel Ruysch
Roses, Convolvulus, Poppies and Other Flowers in an Urn on a Stone Ledge
c. 1745
page 24

Artist unknown
Yam Mask
Nineteenth century
page 110

Visual Index

Artist unknown
Duncan House Bedroom
1805
page 178

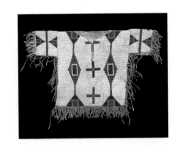

Artist unknown
Child's Beaded Shirt
c. 1865
page 170

Artist unknown
Thunderbird Shield
c. 1830
page 140

Artist unknown
Double Saddlebag
1875
page 28

Artist unknown
Parasol
Mid-nineteenth century
page 157

Artist unknown
Washington's Headquarters
c. 1876
page 81

Albert Edward Edensaw
Dancing Headdress Frontlet
1860–1870
page 111

Edgar Degas
Waiting
c. 1882
page 123

Visual Index

Claude Monet
Bridge over a Pool of Water Lilies
1899
page 17

Artist unknown
Feather Headdress
Early twentieth century
page 136

Artist unknown
Necklace
Twentieth century
page 96

Claude Monet
Water Lilies
1905
page 148

Wassily Kandinsky
Improvisation No. 27
1912
page 20

Allen E. Cole
Silas Johnson
1920s
page 37

Martha Walter
The Telegram, Detention Room, Ellis Island
1922
page 149

Joseph Henry Sharp
Sunset Dance-Ceremony to the Evening Sun
1924
page 33

Visual Index

Paul Klee
Rotes Haus
1929
page 62

Berenice Abbott
Nos. 4, 6, & 8 Fifth Avenue
1936
page 32

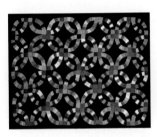

Mrs. Andy G. Byler
Double Wedding Ring Quilt
1930–1940
page 152

Henri Matisse
Purple Robe and Anemones
1937
page 156

Shirley Russell
Boys' Day
1935
page 46

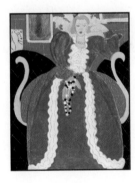

Henri Matisse
Woman in Blue
1937
page 183

Emily Carr
Sky
1935
page 59

Man Ray
La Fortune
1938
page 54

Visual Index

Yves Tanguy
Indefinite Divisibility
1942
page 58

Horace Pippin
Victorian Parlor II
1945
page 106

Philip Evergood
Her World
1948
page 119

Calvin Jones
*Brilliant as the Sun
Upon the World*
c. 1950
page 55

Fernand Léger
The Walking Flower
1951
page 88

Hughie Lee-Smith
The Piper
1953
page 80

Allan Houser
Apache Crown Dance
1953
page 126

Charles Burchfield
Orion in December
1959
page 16

Visual Index

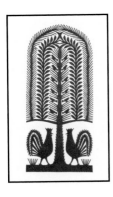

Stanistawa Bakula
Tree of Life
1962
page 77

Alexander Calder
The Spinner
1966
page 89

Ayako Miyawaki
Various Fish
1967
page 141

Joseph Jean-Gilles
Haitian Landscape
1973
page 84

Audrey Flack
Buddha
1975
page 144

Nancy Youngblood Lugo
Pottery Vessels
c. 1980–1985
page 167

Rosalind Ragans
Firebirds
1983
page 63

Isabel John
Pictorial Tapestry
Mid 1980s
page 171

Visual Index

Yvonne Jacquette
Tokyo Street with Pachinko Parlor II
1985
page 122

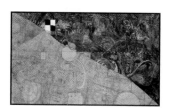

William T. Wiley
Remedial Archaeology and the Like
1986
page 51

© 1988 **Faith Ringgold**
Tar Beach
1988
page 47

Idelle Weber
Pistia Kew
1989
page 66

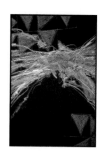

Bing Davis
Ancestral Spirit Dance Series
1990
page 182

Janet Fish
Arcanum
1990
page 25

Sylvia Plimack Mangold
The Locust Trees with Maple
1990
page 85

Jane Freilicher
The Sun Breaks Through
1991
page 127

Iris Sandkühler
*Tuxedo Studs
and Cufflinks*
1994
page 97

Kathryn Gough
Book Cover
1995
page 187

Glossary

alternating rhythm
(ôl tər nā´ ting r̂th´ əm), **noun**

When one motif is repeated after a second, different motif.

appliqué
(ap´ li kā´), **noun**

An art form in which cutout fabrics are attached onto a larger surface.

approximate symmetry
(ə prok´ sə mit sim´ i trē), **noun**

When both sides of a design are *almost* exactly the same. Approximate symmetry is a type of formal balance.

architect
(är´ kə tekt), **noun**

An artist who plans and designs buildings.

architecture
(är´ kə tek´ chûr), **noun**

The art of designing and planning buildings for people.

background
(bak´ ground´), **noun**

The area of the picture that seems farthest from the viewer.

batik
(bə tēk´), **noun**

A way to design fabric using hot wax and dyes.

bookmaking
(bu̇k mā´ king), **noun**

The art of binding or tying pages together inside a cover.

Glossary

center of interest
(sen´ tər əv in´ trist), **noun**

The area of an artwork that a viewer immediately looks at first.

central axis
(sen´ trəl ak´ sis), **noun**

An imaginary line dividing a work of art in half.

color spectrum
(kul´ ər spek´ trəm), **noun**

The range of colors that come from light.

color wheel
(kul´ ər hwēl´), **noun**

A design for organizing colors that shows the spectrum bent into a circle.

complex geometric shape
(kom´ pleks jē´ ə met´ rik shāp), **noun**

A shape made by combining simple geometric shapes such as triangles, squares, and rectangles.

contrast
(kon´ trast), **noun (verb)**

A difference between two things in a work of art.

cool colors
(kül´ kul´ ərz), **noun**

Spectral colors that give a feeling of coolness. Green, blue, and violet are cool colors.

culture
(kul´ chər), **noun**

Another word for *custom.*

curved
(kûrvd), **adj.**

Lines that bend and change direction slowly.

depth
(depth), **noun**

The appearance of distance on a flat surface.

Glossary

diagonal
(dī ag´ ə nəl), **adj. (noun)**

Lines that are slanted.

diamond
(dī´ mənd), **noun**

emphasis
(em´ fə sis), **noun**

The way an artist makes something in a work of art stand out.

exaggerate
(eg zaj´ ə rāt), **verb**

To make much larger than actual size.

foreground
(fôr´ ground´), **noun**

The area of the picture that seems closest to the viewer.

form
(fôrm), **noun**

A three-dimensional object. Forms can be measured in three ways: height, width, and depth.

formal balance
(fôr´ məl bal´ əns), **noun**

A way of organizing a design so that equal or very similar elements are placed on opposite sides of an imaginary, central dividing line.

free-form (shape)
(frē´ fôrm´), **noun**

A shape that is uneven and not regular; a shape that is not geometric.

freestanding
(frē´ stan´ ding), **noun (adj.)**

A three-dimensional sculpture that has empty, negative space all around.

geometric (shape)
(jē´ ə met´ rik), **noun (adj.)**

A math shape, such as a circle, triangle, rectangle, or square.

Glossary

guidelines
(gīd´ līnz´), **noun**

Lines that help an artist place things in a work of art.

harmony
(här´ mə nē), **noun**

The peaceful look made when related elements of art are put together.

hexagon
(hek´ sə gon), **noun**

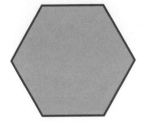

highlight
(hī´ līt´), **noun**

A small area of white used to show the very brightest spot on an object.

horizontal
(hôr´ ə zon´ təl), **adj.**

Lines that are straight across from side to side.

hue
(hū), **noun**

Another word for *color*.

interior designer
(in tîr´ ē ər   di zī´ nər), **noun**

An artist who decorates the insides of buildings using furnishings, such as carpeting, furniture, and drapes.

intermediate color
(in´ tər mē´ dē it   kul´ ər),
noun

A color made by mixing a primary color and a secondary color.

jeweler
(jü´ ə lər), **noun**

An artist who designs and makes jewelry.

jewelry
(jü´ əl rē), **noun**

Three-dimensional art that is made for people to wear.

Glossary

line
(līn), **noun**

A mark drawn by a tool such as a pencil, pen, or paintbrush as it moves across a surface.

line variety
(līn və rī′ ə tē), **noun**

Short or long, thick or thin, rough or smooth, and broken or solid lines.

mask
(mask), **noun**

Three-dimensional art form of a sculpted face.

mosaic
(mō zā′ ik), **noun**

A picture made by setting small pieces of colored tile, glass, or stone side by side.

motif
(mō tēf′), **noun**

A shape or object that is repeated.

negative space
(neg′ ə tiv spās′), **noun**

The empty area around shapes and objects in an artwork.

octagon
(ok′ tə gon), **noun**

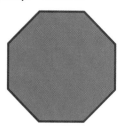

overlap
(ō′ vər lap′), **verb (noun)**

When one object covers part of a second object.

parallelogram
(pâr′ ə lel′ ə gram), **noun**

Glossary

pentagon
(pen´ tə gon), **noun**

portrait
(pôr´ trit), **noun**

A picture of a person.

positive space
(poz´ i tiv spās´), **noun**

The area that shapes and objects fill in a work of art.

primary color
(prī´ mer ē kul´ ər), **noun**

One of the three basic colors: red, yellow, and blue. Primary colors cannot be made by mixing other colors.

random rhythm
(ran´ dəm rith´ əm), **noun**

When a motif is repeated in no particular order.

regular rhythm
(reg´ yə lər rith´ əm), **noun**

Visual rhythm that is created by repeating the same motif with equal amounts of space in between.

relief sculpture
(ri lēf´ skulp´ chər), **noun**

Artwork in which forms stand out from a flat surface.

repetition
(rep´ i tish´ ən), **noun**

When an artist repeats lines, colors, or textures.

sculpture
(skulp´ chər), **noun**

A kind of art that is three-dimensional.

secondary color
(sek´ ən der´ ē kul´ ər), **noun**

A color made by mixing two primary colors.

Glossary

shade
(shād), **noun**

Any dark value of a color.

tactile texture
(tak´ təl teks´ chər), **noun**

The way the surface of an object actually feels when you touch it.

shape
(shāp), **noun**

A flat, two-dimensional area. Shapes can be measured by length and width.

texture
(teks´ chər), **noun**

The way the surface of an object feels or looks as if it would feel.

simplicity
(sim plis´ i tē), **noun**

A method of creating unity by using only one color, shape, or texture in a work of art.

three-dimensional
(thrē´ di men´ shə nəl), **adj. (noun)**

Forms that can be measured by height, width, and depth.

spectral color
(spek´ trəl kul´ ər), **noun**

One of the six colors of the rainbow. Red, orange, yellow, green, blue, and violet are spectral colors.

tint
(tint), **noun**

Any light value of a color.

symmetry
(sim´ i trē), **noun**

A type of formal balance when both halves of a design are identical, mirror images of each other.

trapezoid
(trap´ ə zoid), **noun**

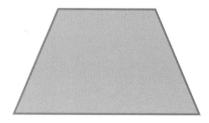

Glossary

two-dimensional
(tü´ di men´ shə nəl), **adj.**
(noun)

Shapes that are flat and can be
measured by length and width.

unity
(ū´ ni tē), **noun**

The feeling of wholeness in a
work of art.

value
(val´ ū), **noun**

The lightness or darkness of a
color.

variety
(və rī´ ə tē), **noun**

The use of different lines, shapes,
colors, and textures to make a
work of art interesting.

vertical
(vûr´ tə kəl), **adj.**

Lines that move straight up and
down.

visual rhythm
(vizh´ ü əl   ri<u>th</u>´ əm), **noun**

The feeling of movement created
by artists repeating colors, shapes,
lines, and textures.

visual texture
(vizh´ ü əl   təks´ chər), **noun**

Texture you see with your eyes
but cannot feel with your hands.

warm colors
(wôrm´   kul´ ərz), **noun**

Spectral colors that give a feeling
of warmth. Yellow, orange, and
red are warm colors.

zigzag
(zig´ zag´), **noun (adj.)**

Diagonal lines that connect.

Index

Index

Index

Index

Index